The Other Side of Hell

Charles Bynum

"The Other Side of Hell" is a true story, however some names and minor details have been changed and some characters have been combined.

The Other Side of Hell
Copyright © 2011 Charles Bynum

All rights reserved.

ISBN: 978-0615690148
ISBN-13: 0615690149

Published by The Divine In Me Publishing, LLC
Colorado Springs, Colorado
Charles.l.bynum@gmail.com

Cover art Copyright © 2011 by Marie David http://mariemdavid.com
Cover Design Copyright © 2011 by Rebecca Davis, Davis Creative

To Tina

CHAPTER ONE

A journey of a thousand miles begins with one step. – Lau Tzu

"How are you feeling today?" Robert asked.

"I'm fine," I replied. His sideways glance told me he didn't believe me. I didn't care.

"It's been nine months now," he probed. He stared patiently, saying nothing, hoping to elicit a response from me. I was not going to give him what he wanted. I knew the silence would cause him far more discomfort than me. He looked down at his notes; a good sign that I was winning. He scribbled something on his notepad, and then, "Have you nothing to say?" he asked at last, unable to bear the silence any longer.

"Success!" I thought. Silly little game I was playing, but it amused me. Poor Robert. He had from the very first made it clear that I was to call him Robert—not Doctor Sanders. No, calling him doctor anything would have been far too impersonal. He wanted me to think of him as my friend.

I stared at him, his white shirt and yellow tie, his relaxed demeanor and salt and pepper hair, his warm smile painted so perfectly on his squarely chiseled face. Here before me sat the image of the caring, compassionate man dedicating his life to helping those like me. And by those like me I mean poor souls who had lost their way, poor souls in need. Yes, good old "Robert" was everything you could ever hope a therapist might be—everything, that is, but real.

"Your last words to me were 'It's been nine months now.' That's not a question," I said. "Technically, you used a sentence fragment, so those words don't even form a complete sentence. I was politely waiting on you to finish your thought." I was playing with him and he knew it. But the facts are what they are, therefore I had him. He knew this too. He smiled. It was a most warm and friendly smile designed to demonstrate how much he really cared and wanted to help me. I wasn't fooled. That smile was nothing but a thin veneer hiding his contempt for my little game and I knew it. This pompous bastard thinks he's better than me. I can see through him though. I know what he's really thinking. Since I don't care I simply smile back, mirroring the same fake smile he's giving me. He leans forward tilting his head slightly, another show of false sincerity. He's laying it on thick today.

"Charles," he says, his voice soft and caring. "It's been nine months that you've been coming to see me and I feel we are not progressing as we should." Now I'm angry. He says *we* are not progressing as *we* should. What he really means is *I* am not progressing as *I* should. I wouldn't hate him so much if he would just say what he really means. The fake, "we" bullshit is supposed to make me think that we are a team; that we are somehow in this together. We are not. I am in it. He is just the observer paid to act like my friend. I don't care how much he wants to act like he understands the torment I have suffered. The fact is he has no clue. He has his textbook examples of what one is supposed to do in such situations without the slightest understanding of what it is really like for *me*.

He's staring at me again, pausing, hoping that I will say something in response. Fuck him.

"Charles," he continues now that he realizes my mouth is glued shut. "I'm worried about our progress here. You're keeping your feelings locked away and not giving them adequate expression. This is not healthy."

My blood boils. I want to shout, "Just who the fuck do you think you are?" Every muscle in my body tightens and I want to jump up and punch this phony bastard, knock that caring look right off his face. But I hold it in. To do that would be to let him win. I cannot let him win. I cannot let him think he got to me. I gather my strength and shove all my anger, all my hatred for this man, back into the depths of my soul from whence it came. I want to kill him…I really do.

"What are you feeling right now, Charles?" he asks.

"Nothing," I lie. I can't possibly tell him that I am fantasizing about the pleasure I would derive by inflicting a slow and agonizing death upon him right here and right now.

"You know, Charles," he continues, "I am not the cause of all this anger you are feeling."

Damn it! How does he know? He can't possibly know. I quickly move to conceal my wide-eyed, open-jawed expression, but it's too late. He saw it; I know he saw it. He's a sneaky son-of-a-bitch, this one. I'll have to be more careful. Crafty bastard. He thinks he got me but he didn't. Just landed a punch, that's all. I can recover from this.

"You're right," I say. "I've been coming here for nine months now and have not been making any real progress. Perhaps your skills as a doctor are less than adequate. A good therapist would have brought about the progress that you seem to think is lacking. The problem is not me, Dr. Sanders, it is you."

"Really?" he replies. "Tell me Charles, how have I failed you?"

"How have you failed me? How have you failed me? All I've heard from you is 'You need to open up, Charles. You need to express your feelings, Charles. You need to let it all out, Charles.' Well fuck you and fuck my feelings! You don't know what it's like. You don't know what I've been through. You think you know, but you don't."

"Tell me, Charles, what *is* it like for you? What *have* you been through?"

"Have you not been listening?" I shout. "I've been coming here week after week telling you. You don't listen! You don't care! Everything about you is fake and phony. You act like you're my friend but you're not." I am in a rage now and I am spewing my wrath upon him. I'm doubly pissed because I didn't want this to happen. He made it happen. I hate him. I can't sit still any longer. I have to get out of here.

"I've had enough of this shit!" I shout. "I'm leaving!" I storm out of his office, slamming the door behind me.

• • •

That was how it all began. That was the day I first started to unravel. My life, from that moment on, would never be the same. I had begun my descent into the maelstrom. Good old Dr. Sanders, Robert, popped the cork out of the bottle that day, and try as I might, I would never get the damned thing back in.

I have many times been asked by otherwise normal people to explain the insanity of addiction. What, they ask, would make a successful, well-educated man of forty-two years of age go so completely insane? To this question I can give no reasonable answer, because the truth is, I cannot begin to understand it myself. The best I can do is describe it. I can carry you through it affording you a glimpse into the insanity. Perhaps then you will be able to experience the insanity in such a way as to come to some understanding on your own.

The descent into addiction actually comes quite easily. It is the journey back that is difficult. I was a successful businessman leading what, by anyone's standards, was a reasonably successful life. I had the requisite home, two cars, a wife and a child that every American was supposed to have. Then, in a moment, everything changed. The wife and child were suddenly gone; doesn't matter how, doesn't matter why. They were simply gone, and everything that ever meant anything suddenly meant nothing. I became like a ship whose moors had snapped and I was drifting aimlessly about…strangely detached from life.

Strangely detached from life. What an understatement. I had heard of people succumbing to depression, but I thought all of that was foolishness. "Chemical imbalance of the brain my ass," I thought. These were weak-willed people who had given up on life. A swift kick in the butt was what these people needed. Then it happened to me. How can I describe the despair, the utter hopelessness that invaded my soul and sucked all of the color, all of the texture, all of the joy from my life? It sneaks up on you, and by the time you realize it has you, it's too late. Before you know it, you find yourself not really living, not really dead. You are in some surreal limbo, a purgatory from which you see your life without really experiencing your life. The vibrant, colorful world comes through in hazy shades of gray. Sounds seem muffled and distant, utterly uninteresting. Food tastes bland. Your skin feels soft, spongy. It is an agony beyond agony, a total and absolute disconnect from the organic, living world. You are thrust into a nightmarish existence from which there is no hope of escape. Alone, lost in a despair darker than the blackest black, your body goes numb.

This darkness breeds a subtle desperation that grows like a cancer in the soul. Death seems less a terrible end and more a welcome relief. Even simple tasks like getting out of bed in the morning become a chore; the weight of continued existence bearing down unmercifully upon you, sapping every last ounce of strength. From the depths of despair you try to force yourself to continue living, yet you find yourself instead going through the motions of life with a disinterested sadness from which you can derive no meaning, no purpose, no reason to continue. You see others who seem to be enjoying their lives, and you would hate them if you could muster the energy to hate. But you cannot. Even hate requires a degree of engagement with life, an engagement that utterly eludes you. Life seems patently absurd—a race toward the inevitable death that awaits us all, with nothing but suffering between then and now. Sure there are moments of joy and pleasure, but these are little more than punctuation marks. Suffering is the dialog. Suffering is the discourse. Suffering is life.

From this darkness, drug use seems a reasonable alternative. Break your leg and the doctor will give you drugs to ease your pain. Break your life and they offer nothing but words. My life was broken, and words only increased the pain. I wanted to end the pain, and if I had to die to do so—well, that seemed a reasonable alternative. The only alternative that did not seem reasonable was healing, because healing seemed an impossible proposition. I was suffering from the terminal disease known as life, and as such, I had but two options—end the disease, or medicate the pain.

CHAPTER TWO

By three methods we may learn wisdom: First, by reflection, which is noblest; Second, by imitation, which is easiest; and third by experience, which is the bitterest. – Confucius

My friend Brandon had been hounding me for weeks to get out of the house and do something, anything, with him. This was, of course, something I was loathe to do. My depression made getting out of bed the most difficult of chores. Going anywhere was unthinkable. But Brandon was persistent. I finally relented and agreed to attend a party some friends of his were having in their home. It was there that I first met Heather.

"What the hell is bothering you?" she asked in the rude manner I would come to know as her normal means of communication. Tact was not her strong suit. The question caught me off guard.

I stared at her for a moment without answering. I wanted her to go away, to leave me alone with my drink. "Hey, I'm talking to you," she persisted; then she smiled. Something about her smile and the sparkle in her bright, blue eyes penetrated the fog of my existence. It was as if something that had been slumbering in the deepest depths of my soul stirred ever so slightly—it didn't wake, mind you—but, at long last, it moved.

"What do you mean?" I replied dully.

Her head tilted slightly to the right and her eyes widened. She seated herself on the sofa beside me and leaned in close. "You know," she said, "this *is* a party, and people are *supposed* to have fun at parties."

"I am having fun," I lied while staring at my drink.

"Oh…well…if this is you having fun, I would hate to imagine what you're like on a bad day." She smiled, obviously pleased by her remark. I, however, was not so pleased.

"Why are you talking to me?" I asked coldly.

"Sorry!" she replied as she leaned away from me, her head tilting downward until her chin nearly touched her chest. "Aren't you the friendly one?" She was not offended; she was simply feigning offense in her playful little way. I didn't care. I dropped my head and stared into my glass. "I'll tell you what, *love*," she continued, and as she spoke, she touched my left leg just above the knee. My eyes reflexively darted to her hand and my body went defensively stiff. "I'm going to leave you alone so you can continue to make love to your misery." She paused, narrowing her eyes as if to drive her words deep into my heart. It was as if she was saying to me, "I see you," without actually saying it. Then she simply stood and walked away.

I continued to stare at my drink, but soon my eyes took on a life of their own. They kept glancing at this unusual woman. I struggled to resist, but my eyes would not cooperate. They kept finding their way back to Heather. She was beautiful, slim, with shoulder-length blonde hair. But that was not what captured my attention. It was the vibrance of her energy that kept calling my eyes to her. She flitted about the room, smiling and talking with a careless ease. This woman seemed so very alive; and I felt so very dead.

"I see you've met Heather." Brandon had suddenly materialized beside me.

"Uh…oh, yeah…I suppose I kinda did," I replied. "Heather, you say? So that's her name?"

"Charles, come on. I saw you here talking to her. You didn't even ask her name?"

I shifted nervously in my seat. "No…I suppose I didn't. Didn't think to ask, to tell you the truth."

"Man, you are way out of practice, aren't you?" My friend Brandon meant well, but as was often the case, he was irritating the hell out of me.

"I'm not interested in that kind of thing," I said sharply.

"Charles," he said leaning toward me, his voice lowering. "We are all interested in that kind of thing." He smiled knowingly and nudged my arm with his elbow. Despite my best efforts, a smile slowly crept over my face. "You should go talk to her," Brandon continued.

"Noooo," I protested. "What would she want with someone like me? I must be twenty years older than her."

"There's no harm in talking to her," he continued. "There's no telling what might happen if you talk to her. But nothing will happen if you don't. That's a guarantee." He smiled at me as he stood.

"Get out of here," I said as I waved him away.

"Suit yourself, my friend. Maybe you'll get lucky and that glass you keep staring at will go home with you this evening." His laughter told me he thought himself quite funny. I sat shaking my head, as he walked away in search of someone else to grace with his drunken presence.

Funny thing about life. We like to think we are in control of everything we do, yet sometimes life moves us in the direction it wants us to go despite ourselves. This was one such moment. It was as if some universal intelligence was moving me ever so subtly toward a particular outcome. We often miss these things because we are so shackled by our concepts of good and bad. This was to be a "bad" outcome, therefore, the intelligence of the universe could not possibly want me to go in that direction, right? Wrong. This thinking is short sighted. Life has lessons to teach us, and toward that end it often moves us toward suffering so that we might learn. This, I believe, was my invitation into just such a journey. There I was staring at an empty glass; and there Heather was, standing alone at the bar, her left hand gently tugging at the curls in her long blonde hair. I'd like to tell you that it was some strong attraction to this woman that motivated me. I'd like to tell you that I wanted to get to know her better, that I was tired of being lonely and thought she would make interesting company. I would like to tell you all of that, but I can't. That would be a lie. The truth is that I have no idea what made me get up and walk over to that bar. But I did. Something simply took over and I found myself walking toward her. Heather's eyes met mine as I approached, and a very strange thing happened inside me. My normal approach would be to slightly smile at her, and then look away as if mildly disinterested. But not this time. My eyes locked onto hers and I held them there. I felt that strange sense of absolute confidence born of hopelessness; born from the fact that I did not care about anything. There was a certain freedom in it. I felt a sudden surge of power as if I could do anything I wanted, and what I wanted in that moment was her. I did not walk up beside her as if to fill my glass; I instead walked straight to her and stood silently before her, my eyes locked with hers, my gaze telling her that I wanted her, and that I would have her.

"*Well*...what got into you?" she asked, playfully.

I said nothing.

Heather smiled knowingly. She stopped tugging at her curls and let her hand drop to her side. Her eyes sparkled. "Come with me," she said as she took my hand and led me away. We passed through the crowded room and went down a hallway that led to the bathroom. "In here," she said, as she pulled me in and closed the door, locking it behind us. She retrieved from her bra a small plastic baggie about one inch square. I saw within it a crystalline like substance.

"You're going to like this," she said with a sly grin.

She poured a small amount of the substance out onto the bathroom counter, retrieved a blue cigarette lighter from her purse, and used the side of the lighter to crush the shards into a fine powder. I cannot tell you what I was thinking. Most likely, I was not thinking at all. It was as if events were unfolding, and I was simply along for the ride. I knew I would do whatever this young woman asked of me. This is the most important thing to realize. As I said before, sometimes life imposes itself upon a person. I think I am making a conscious choice, but in reality, I am simply being carried along to wherever life wants me to go. What I did not know then was that this was the beginning of a journey; a journey that would at times seem like an excursion into hell. It was a moment in which, as much as I would like to say I made a choice, as much as I would like to believe I should have chosen differently, there was no choice. Life was simply carrying me along into the transformative horror that would ultimately mold me into the man I was to become. And life, in its infinite wisdom, knew to use my carnal nature to drive me where it wanted me to go. At the time, however, I could think only of one thing—I wanted this woman.

She retrieved a credit card from her purse and began dividing the powder, shaping it into four neat little lines. She moved with expert precision and a smoothness that told me she had done this many times before. She then began digging around in the bottom of her purse, and in a few moments, retrieved a small piece of soda straw about three inches long. "Cheers," she said with a smile, then proceeded to snort the substance into her nose; one line in the left nostril, the other line in the right.

She tilted her head back sharply, her eyes watering slightly. "Wow!" she said as she brought her head back down. She blinked deliberately a few times and handed me the straw. "Your turn," she said, a knowing smile painted across her face.

"How am I supposed to do this?" I asked. She looked up at me, her eyes widening slightly at the realization that I had never done this before. She had the good taste to say nothing about it.

"Put the straw in one nostril and close the other with your finger," she instructed. I did as she told me and leaned toward the counter, the straw touching the bottom of the first line. I let out my breath so I could snort the line, but my exhalation scattered the powder, blowing it all over the counter.

"Hold on," she said with a wide grin on her face indicating that this was a common mistake made by those who had never done this before. She took her credit card and began reshaping the lines. "I forgot to tell you. Let your breath out *before* you lower your head, and that won't happen."

"Sorry," I said.

"No worries, happens all the time," she responded. "Oh, and one more thing, do both lines quickly. Snort the first line in your left nostril, then quickly snort the other in your right."

I nodded, let out my breath *before* leaning over to the countertop, and proceeded to snort both lines exactly as she instructed. My head reflexively jolted upright and tears streamed from my eyes. Funny thing about snorting methamphetamine, the shit burns like fire. I felt as if I had snorted molten lava into my nose. My breath came in short, rapid gasps in response to the intense pain.

"Relax," Heather reassured me, "the burning only lasts a few moments." She was correct. The burning had already begun to subside and was quickly tapering off to nothing. Heather looked up at me smiling with anticipation.

The effect was instant. I felt an incredible surge of liquid electricity racing through my body. My skin tingled, my heart fluttered, and I gasped slightly to catch my breath. A wave of euphoria flooded my brain with an intense pleasure unlike anything I had ever experienced before. I was on fire! But unlike the burning in my nostrils from a moment before, this was an energetic fire of extreme pleasure engulfing my entire being. It carried with it a sense of power and confidence. It was electric, exciting. I loved it!

Heather smiled broadly. "Yeah? yeah?" she asked while nodding her head.

"Oh yeah!" I replied heavily, smiling back at her. A sudden surge of power engulfed me. I could do anything. The world was mine for the taking. My eyes locked onto Heather's. Her eyes widened with eager anticipation, and my desire for her seared through my body. I slid my arm around her waist and yanked her into me forcefully. I wasn't asking; I was taking. I kissed her deeply, powerfully, and began sliding her dress up over her hips as she frantically loosened my belt and fumbled with my zipper. I grabbed her panties and yanked them to her ankles and she quickly stepped out of them. I dropped my pants down to my knees, grabbed her shoulders, spun her around and bent her over the bathroom counter. I did not "make love" to her that evening. I did not "have sex" with her. I fucked her. It was something primal, animal, violent. I took what I wanted, no apologies, no excuses. She was mine to do with as I willed. It was my pure carnal nature fueled by meth-induced adrenaline, unleashed and amplified a thousand fold…

Thus began my descent into the madness. Looking back I realize that there are two things about methamphetamine that make it so powerfully addictive. First, you don't feel intoxicated like you do with other drugs. If anything, methamphetamine produces an effect that is the antithesis of intoxication. You feel more alert, more alive. And along with that sensation comes the absolute cure for pain. I did not realize it at the time, but from the moment the drug hit my brain, my depression evaporated. There was no sorrow, no sadness while meth surged through my veins.

The second thing I came to understand was something you never hear anyone talk about. Drug addiction is intricately woven into the same neural fibers in the brain as the sex drive. In retrospect I see that drug and alcohol use more often than not accompanied my sexual encounters. I learned early on that a few drinks lowered my inhibitions, and that made it easier to approach women. I have come to believe that the drive to use drugs is essentially the same as the drive to have sex. It is as if the two fuse into one. People who get clean often speak of how difficult and awkward it is to have sex sober. It is as if they have to re-learn how to do it minus the drug. Yes, we often hear of sex and drugs, as if the two belong together. We are woefully unaware of just how "together" the two actually are.

Heather came home with me that first night, and from then on, we were inseparable. The meth world is like that. You are suddenly best friends with a perfect stranger. I knew nothing about Heather, and yet I thought she was the greatest woman who ever lived. It is important to note that this feeling had nothing to do with her. It was meth that fooled me into thinking she was so wonderful. The drug stimulated the pleasure centers of my brain, and I associated that pleasure with her. This is the insidious nature of methamphetamine. Your mind can no longer be trusted because it is making associations based upon artificial stimulation. It's like throwing a chemical wrench into the gears of your brain.

Heather became my entrance into a new world. A door opened, and I couldn't help but to step through. What I found on the other side was a place I call Tweakerville.

Tweakerville is not like an ordinary town. You cannot find it on any map. In fact, you can't find it at all; it finds you. It has always been there, right in front of your eyes, though it is unlikely that you have ever seen it. It exists everywhere and it exists nowhere. It is a strange and surreal place hovering just beneath the surface of normal life. It is more like a portal to some alternate dimension of reality; a dimension intricately interwoven into the cloth of the normal world. It invites you in with its devilish allure. It is an intoxicating place of seduction, danger and exquisite darkness. Once it reveals itself to you, you can suddenly see it everywhere. Its siren's call lures you in, and as with the sirens of old, the price you pay for admittance is your soul.

My introduction to this madness began as one never-ending party. Heather came with me to my home. She was moving in, though neither of us bothered to discuss this. We didn't even take time to think about it. It was simply assumed—or rather, it just happened. Heather was on her cell phone before we even made it back to my house, calling all of her friends and cohorts. Before I knew it, my home suffered from an infestation of tweakers.

For those who do not know, a tweaker is a meth addict. If you are high on meth, you are said to be "tweaking." The term originated from the fact that people rarely sleep when using the drug. It is not uncommon for a user to stay awake for two weeks at a stretch, therefore they began to be called "two-weekers." Over time, this label was combined into the term "tweaker." There are other words I would come to know that were part of the tweaker vernacular. One I learned rather quickly was the term "falling out." This was an interesting phenomenon. It seems that the human body has a natural shutting down mechanism that no amount of meth can prevent. After about fourteen days of constant tweaking with no sleep whatsoever, the user literally falls into a sudden, deep stupor from which he cannot be aroused, and it can last for days. There is nothing to do but leave him where he is until he wakes up.

Once the tweakers moved in, my home was overrun with strange and unusual people, all of whom were a part of the tweaker world. This was a unique sub-culture of people. Some were ordinary folks who held down regular jobs and just dipped in from time to time, but most were transients who never held any fixed place of residence. They simply drifted from location to location, spending a day here and a day there. A few had homes, and they were the ones who played host to the many other tweakers who were continually coming and going. Since I was new to the scene and I had a home, I was a host. What I did not realize at the time was the truly parasitic nature of these people.

CHAPTER THREE

The fool who persists in his folly will become wise. – William Blake

"Look at this shit," Ben said excitedly. Ben was twenty-seven years old. He had blonde hair, cropped very short. He wore what I had come to refer to as the standard tweaker uniform: baggy pants, loose shirt and a cap turned backwards on his head. He held in his hand a loaded meth pipe. A meth pipe is basically a four inch long glass tube about a half inch in diameter. One end of the pipe has been formed into a glass ball about one inch across. There is a small opening on the top of the glass ball for air to enter when you inhale from the cylindrical end of the pipe. The meth is loaded into the ball end of the pipe, and heat from a lighter is applied.

"Look at that," he said as he held the pipe with the now liquid dope that had melted under his expert hand. "See how it turned blue? That means this is some really good shit."

I had learned that not all meth was equal. It was given different names depending upon its specific characteristics, such as "lemon drop" for meth that came as yellow shards, or "skittles" which turned different colors as it was heated. This new dope of Ben's was the skittles variety. As the pipe was passed around, the dope first turned a brilliant blue, then purple, then a deep aquatic green, finally ending up orange as the last bit vaporized.

I sat watching the people who had gathered in my house. We were in a circle in my living room, passing the pipe around and chatting incessantly about meaningless things. Heather was sitting next to me on my right, Ben was on my left. Next to Ben was a thirty-nine year old Mexican man nicknamed Spider. Tweakers love their silly little nicknames. Not all of them used such names, but many did. Spider's girlfriend, Nichole, was sitting next to him.

Smoking meth was, in its own strange way, a kind of social event. This in itself had a strange allure. Tweakers don't watch television. They instead gather in groups, pass the pipe around and talk. And they would do this for hours—usually all night long, in fact. I remember thinking how nice it was to have real social interaction again. We shared a common bond, and these people all seemed to me to be my friends. I felt a part of something again and I loved it.

I observed these strange people as they went about their unusual ritual. I was lost to the allure of the meth world. It seemed to be the answer to my loneliness, to my depression; the antidote to my recent suffering. And yet, this life was nothing but suffering. These people were not happy, not content. Their lives were utterly empty. The drug was their escape, their coping mechanism, the cure for pain. It was too easy. Problems were never dealt with. They were simply smoked away. The pain of life dissolved into a cloud of smoke. It was a strangely surreal existence in which one simply floated about in a fog which no problem could penetrate.

When Ben handed me the pipe, I took my lighter and began heating the dope. This is a very delicate procedure. You must heat it enough to liquefy it, but if you over heat it, it will burn transforming into a bitter tasting concoction which will immediately spark the full wrath of everyone in the room. I had learned this lesson the hard way, and was now very careful not to burn the dope. I held the lighter beneath the round ball and slowly twisted the pipe back and forth to evenly distribute the heat. Soon it began to liquefy and I backed the flame off a bit; close enough to keep the dope liquid, but not so close that the dope would burn. I continued twisting the pipe as I brought it to my lips. I inhaled deeply and did so for as long as possible, filling every inch of space in my lungs with smoke. When I could take in no more, I removed the flame and held my breath, allowing the drug to move through my lungs and into my bloodstream. When I could hold my breath no longer, I exhaled a huge cloud of smoke. The dope in the pipe almost immediately solidified once the heat was removed, another sign of superior quality. Good dope solidifies quickly; lesser dope stays liquid longer.

"Damn, that is some good shit," I said as a wave of liquid energy flooded over my body. I felt a tingling sensation all over my skin and my heart raced.

"Look at those legs," Ben said as he pointed to the pipe. "Legs" was a term referring to yet another quality of good dope. When the drug cools in the pipe, most of it settles in a glob at the bottom, but tentacles sometimes remain, reaching up the sides of the pipe. These tentacles are called "legs." These legs occur because the drug solidifies so quickly after the heat is removed that it leaves squiggly trails of dope down the side of the pipe. Just as the best wine exhibits legs when swirled around in a wine glass, the very best dope exhibits this characteristic. Ben's dope was clearly the best and he was quite proud. He pointed out every nuance of his dope as the pipe was passed around. This was Ben's tweak.

Most people have their own particular tweak. A tweak is a habit you begin to obsessively display when you are high on the drug. One very common tweak is to decide that some electronic device is in need of repair. People who display this tweak are forever tearing apart television sets, stereos, DVD players and the like in an attempt to repair some perceived malfunction. They will spend hours disassembling anything they can get their hands on. They never actually repair anything. They simply take it apart, always meaning to put it back together but never actually doing so.

Tweaks also tend to be gender specific. While disassembling electronic devices is something men frequently do, I saw many women pull out coloring books and colored pencils spending hours coloring the pictures. Then there were the carpet sharks. These people were obsessed with the idea that shards of meth had been dropped on the carpet, so they would meticulously comb every inch, parting the carpet with their hands, looking for any stray piece of meth. They looked like monkeys grooming one another in search of lice, except that it was carpet these people groomed. Anything could be a tweak. They were drug induced obsessive-compulsive behaviors.

Some tweaks were not so harmless. For example, many people obsessively picked at their skin. Scab covered arms and legs bore silent witness to the fact that they continually picked at things that were not there. I once saw a girl cutting into her arm with a knife, convinced that there was a sliver of glass stuck in it. She was mutilating herself in an attempt to remove the imaginary sliver.

My tweak, if you could even call it that, was to sit back and observe these people as they engaged in their strange little obsessions. And they are people. They are lost souls. This is the fact that seems to be lost on most people. Those who fall into addiction are people just like anyone else. The difference is that they are lost in an insanity from which they cannot escape. Once the demon addiction wraps its icy arms around you, it will not let go. You become its prisoner, and your every waking moment is spent feeding the beast. It is a lonely existence. You feel completely alone in a room full of people.

"Hey Spider…Spider…" Spider had slumped in his seat and was now sound asleep. His girlfriend Nichole sat hitting the pipe, unconcerned. She then exhaled a cloud of smoke.

"He fell out," Nichole said. "He's been up for days." She handed the pipe to Heather. Ben kept nudging him. "Leave him alone, Ben," Nichole said. "It's no use anyway. He won't move until tomorrow. He does this all the time."

Heather began drawing on the pipe. Spider was suddenly gone. He had withdrawn from the party, from life. He would sleep without moving until the following afternoon. Tweakers are like that.

"You know, we should go do something," Heather said after exhaling a large cloud of white smoke. "I want to get out and go somewhere."

"We'll go wherever you want," I replied, knowing full well that we would not be going anywhere. Another trait of tweakers is that they continually plan things they will never actually do.

"I want to go see a movie," Heather continued.

"Sure thing," I answered. "You find what you want to see, then we'll go."

Heather's eyes were solid black disks. Only dilated pupil existed where her beautiful blue eyes had been. She was wasted now and not thinking clearly. I noticed her picking at her left arm.

"Stop that," I said as I held her hand. "You're going to hurt yourself."

It was no use. The obsession had her and she would pick at her skin until the sun came up the next morning. Her arms were covered with scabs where she had done this numerous times before. This was her tweak, her meth-induced obsession. There was nothing I could do, so I stopped trying.

This is how it went. Gatherings of random people passing the pipe, engaging in banal conversation, doing nothing, going nowhere. At the time this all seemed like such fun. Nothing in my life was actually pleasurable, but the drug stimulated the pleasure centers of the brain, and all of this empty, hollow nothingness felt like the time of my life. That was the insidious lie. The brain was chemically stimulated into feeling pleasure, and it associated that pleasure with my surroundings. Nothing in the world seemed more pleasurable to me than these gatherings which, today in my right mind, would literally drive me mad with boredom.

CHAPTER FOUR

In a controversy the instant we feel anger we have already ceased striving for the truth, and have begun striving for ourselves.
– The Buddha

"Hello Charles," Robert said with his plastic smile. "It's been awhile since our last meeting. How have you been?"

"I've been fine," I replied. "Feeling much better, in fact."

"That's good, I'm glad to hear it."

I can't explain why I continued seeing Robert. It had become a twisted form of self torture, I suppose. I still hated the man, but the hate had been somehow numbed. It was less intense than it had been before.

"Are you ready to start talking about the situation with your wife?" he asked.

This is when I noticed a strange shift inside me. Normally his probing would set me off, but now it didn't bother me as much. I did not yet realize it, but because meth numbed my pain, his questions did not hurt like they had before.

"You already know the story," I said dryly.

"Yes, I do. You have spoken of what happened, but you have never discussed how you felt about it. I would like to hear you speak to that issue."

I thought about his statement. I felt the old anger as I had always felt it when he asked such questions, but it was not as intense as it had been before. This time it seemed as if I could move through it. I began to realize that my anger was a response to the pain. Now that the pain was less, the anger was less also.

"What do you want to know?" I asked.

Robert's gaze shifted almost imperceptibly, but it was enough for me to know that he had been waiting for this moment. "What I want to know is," he said cautiously, "what did you feel when you walked in on your wife and caught her in your bed with another man?"

I felt my anger rise, but it was different this time. It was distant, as if it was happening to someone else. It was like a flame that had no heat. I could run my hand through it and not get burned. I could play with it, toy with it, examine it with impunity. I leaned forward in my seat, my mind fixed on the memory of that day.

"The truth of the matter, Robert," I said slowly, deliberately, "was that I didn't feel anything."

"Nothing?" Robert asked surprised.

I thought for a moment, then I looked straight into Robert's eyes. "I always thought I would kill someone if I found myself in that situation," I said, " but what actually happened was I went dead inside. It was as if the entire thing was more than my body could handle and I just shut down. I turned around and walked out without saying a word."

"Really?" Robert said.

"Really," I replied.

"What about all this anger you demonstrate in here with me?"

I thought about his question. Anger had become the only thing I could feel any more. It was the only emotion that felt safe.

"That came later," I replied.

"Have you been able to feel anything but anger since then?" he asked.

"No," I said and a tear formed in the corner of my right eye. This surprised me because I wasn't aware that I was feeling anything. It was a strange little tear. It was hollow, flat. It seemed strangely disconnected from the living, breathing me; for there no longer seemed to be a living, breathing me. I felt a door opening in the depths of my being, and a wave of terror suddenly came over me. I was feeling something I had not felt before and I didn't like it. The flame of my anger found its heat again and began searing my soul.

"This is good," Robert said. "It is time to begin to reconnect to those emotions that you have buried beneath your anger, Charles."

I hated him again. I felt a wave of anxiety that was nearly unbearable. The bastard had tricked me again and I knew it. Panic set in. I had to get a grip on this; I had to close that door. It felt as though my life depended on it.

"I have to run to the restroom," I said, and I headed out, with Robert calling after me.

I locked the door to the restroom and immediately retrieved my baggie of meth. I quickly crushed two lines onto the counter and snorted them. In seconds, my pain subsided and my anger subsided along with it. I was in control again. I would be fine.

"Sorry about that," I said as I returned to Robert's office. I sat and smiled. "Now where were we?" My calmness had returned, but there was a slight tremor in my right hand. I forced my hand down into the chair beside me so as to hide this from Robert. I didn't want him to know about my drug use.

Robert continued his probing. "I was telling you that I thought it was good that you are beginning to reconnect with the feelings hidden beneath your anger."

"Oh, I see," I said. "I guess that *is* a good thing." I was high now, and numb. The memory of the pain I almost allowed myself to feel was gone. I could do this; I could speak about these things now. "What would you like to know Robert?" I asked.

"Well…" he said, considering his words carefully. "You walked in on her and then walked away feeling nothing. What happened next?"

I stared hard into Robert's eyes. "That was when the darkness set in," I said, my words as dead and lifeless as my life had become. "I stopped caring about anything." I paused to think about what I just said. "That's actually not quite right," I continued. "I was no longer able to care about anything. It was then that I realized that my entire life was nothing but one big lie. My wife moved out and eventually divorced me. I didn't fight at all—I had no fight left in me. She took what she wanted and ran off with her new guy. They left the state, and that was that."

Robert quietly waited for me to continue, but I could think of nothing more to say. After a pause that seemed to last forever, he spoke. "What about your daughter?" he asked.

I looked up at Robert, surprised and puzzled by the question. I hadn't even thought to mention my daughter. What a person does not talk about often says far more than the things he does. What I wasn't saying spoke volumes.

"What about her?" I replied.

"What happened to her?" Robert asked.

A very strange and unusual agony took hold of me. It was an amalgam of shame, guilt and remorse. "She went with her mother," I replied.

"Do you see her at all, talk to her?"

"No."

"Why not?"

I inhaled deeply and sighed heavily. I would have cried if I had the ability to connect to anything still living within me. The emotions swirling around in me were a curious thing. They were a part of me, and yet, they were distant from me.

"There was no fight left in me," I said weakly.

"Do you love your daughter?" Robert asked.

"Yes," I answered.

"Do you have visitation rights?"

"Yes."

"I don't understand, Charles."

How could I explain what I myself did not understand? I loved my daughter more than I loved anything, yet even that love was not enough. I had descended into a darkness so black that nothing could stir me to act. The love of my own child was not sufficient to motivate me into action. I made no attempt to see her, no attempt to talk to her. I removed her completely from my life. To see her would require that I live again, and I was dead. I knew my behavior to be hurtful to her, yet I could do nothing to overcome it. I felt incredible shame. I could not bring myself to believe that I was capable of such a thing, but here I was doing the very thing I would have despised in others. I could not fathom what I had become.

"I don't understand it either, Robert," I said, and as I spoke, I felt my body stiffen and become hard.

"You've had no contact with her since then?" he asked.

"None."

Robert leaned forward in his chair. "There are times," he said, "when people suffer such great emotional trauma that they are incapable, for a time, of giving anything to others. I want you to know, Charles, that in time, as you begin to heal, you will find the ability to re-establish your relationship with your daughter."

"What kind of man abandons his own child?" I asked, as a tear once again formed in the corner of my eye.

"The kind of man who is in so much pain that he simply cannot be there for his daughter right now," he answered.

"I...I can't do this right now," I said as I fought an urge to cry so strong that even the methamphetamine was failing to keep it at bay.

"It's okay, Charles," Robert replied. "You can heal from this. There is still hope."

At that moment I wanted to tell Robert everything. I wanted to tell him about the pain, the agony, the despair. I wanted to tell him about the guilt I felt over my inability to be there for my daughter. I wanted to tell him about the shame I was suffering over the realization that I was no longer a man I could respect. I wanted to tell him about Heather and my drug use. But I could not. I was weak, and I hated myself for it. People like me do not deserve to live, I thought, and I was hell-bent on imposing the punishment I knew I deserved. I was not the man I thought myself to be, and I could not face this simple fact. I had nothing left but a life I could not bear to live, and a drug that forever condemned me to live it anyway. I was bound to my torment, and the drug seemed my only salvation.

"I...I can't..." I said softly, resignedly, and I stood and walked out of Robert's office.

I never told Robert about any of the things that were tormenting me. In fact, I never saw Robert again after that day. I had learned what I needed to know—meth helped me keep it together. Meth helped ease my pain so that I could cope with the realities of my life. Meth had become my friend, my confidant, my therapist, and in it I had found the solution to all life's problems. What need had I for a therapist now?

Robert had done everything right. It is a fact that people are only able to hear when they are ready. I was not ready for what Robert was trying to tell me. Everything I thought myself to be had been ripped away, and I was left with nothing but my suffering. What I know now and didn't know then was how much

I wanted to hang on to that suffering. It defined me. I wrapped myself in it like some infected blanket that caused me nothing but pain, yet was strangely comforting just the same. I was actively choosing that which I thought had been inflicted upon me. This is the inexplicable essence of addiction. The pain of life becomes confused with the suffering of life. Rather than heal from the pain, the addict chooses to continue his suffering. He laments over how unfair it was, how painful it was, and uses this as an excuse he then uses to continue his addiction. It is an absolutely self-reinforcing cycle that serves only to drive one deeper into the abyss. Yet he always feels like it is being done to him. The addict is blind to the fact that it is by his own hand that he suffers.

Looking back, I wish I had done things differently that day. The door to my soul, to my inner pain had to open. I was merely delaying the inevitable. But at the time, the idea of doing so was unthinkable. I was caught in a cycle of running from life, of avoiding pain at all costs by doing that which was sure to bring about the very pain I sought to escape. This is insanity, pure and simple, yet the addict—the one suffering this insanity—is painfully unaware that he is insane. To the addict, irrational choices seem a perfectly rational response to life.

I made an insane choice that day though I didn't realize it. It was a choice that would carry with it terrible consequences. A choice that set me on a path toward total destruction.

Charles Bynum

CHAPTER FIVE

A man who has not passed through the inferno of his passions has never overcome them. – Carl Jung

Life had become one never-ending party, and the changes in me were dramatic. I no longer felt the need to work; no longer felt the need to pay my bills. I no longer felt the need to do any of the things that life requires. But that is not entirely accurate. I knew these things needed to be done, but I found myself always putting them off, always telling myself I would get to them later. Of course, later never came. It was like procrastination on steroids.

There was a strange disconnect in my mind. It was as if my intentions were enough; I never actually had to act. And somehow, in my drug induced insanity, I felt as if the looming consequences of my inaction were unfair. I even managed to shove from my mind the thought that the consequences would ever manifest. It was as if I knew there would be a day of reckoning, but I never fully believed that day would come. This is what the drug does to the mind. My actions no longer seemed in any way connected to the consequences that would inevitably follow. This is how an addict maintains the illusion that he is a perpetual victim of life's inequities without ever recognizing himself as the cause.

It was this disconnect that allowed me to continue on my path. This seems to be a common behavior among addicts. It is like driving a car full-speed toward a concrete wall. You see the wall coming, yet somehow you cannot fully believe it is there. Then, when the inevitable crash comes, you lie bleeding in the wreckage and wonder how such a terrible fate could have befallen you. To those who have never experienced it, no rational explanation can make sense of it. It is supremely irrational. It is, by any definition, a form of absolute insanity. The person caught in this insanity completely believes himself to be a victim of the unfairness of life, while at the same time he knows himself to be the cause of this so-called unfairness. The sufferer experiences this as a split in his brain in which both thoughts are operating at once, and neither thought ever fully communicates with the other.

A healthy person speaking to me at the time would have been confronted with one or the other of these persons possessing my mind. This is what is so confusing to normal people. Speak to me one day and you will be speaking to a man filled with guilt and remorse for the things he is doing to his life. Come back another day, and you will encounter a man who feels himself a victim of life, who cannot help but do the things he is doing. Your initial thought would be to think I am lying and being manipulative. And in a way you would be correct in this assumption. However, the addict is not *exactly* lying. There is a break in his mind that does not allow the conflicting thoughts to be seen together. They never exist at the same time, and the memory of the one is forgotten when the other comes to the fore. You might think that the addict has control over this behavior. He doesn't.

But what about the blatant lying—the lying the addict is fully aware of? This activity is also a part of the addict mind. The addict will tell any lie, betray any friend, cheat, steal, do whatever he must to keep feeding his addiction. The drug is of paramount importance; he will do whatever is necessary to continue to get more. Normal people are limited by feelings of guilt and shame when they betray a friend. The addict is not affected by such feelings because they disappear the moment the drug enters the bloodstream. Imagine what it would be like if every breath of air cost you money. Soon you would run out of money having spent it on the breathing you had already done. You are now letting out your final breath and you have no idea where the money for the next one will come from. The desperation you would feel would become so great that you would do anything to secure that next breath. The addict becomes as desperate for that next fix as you would be awaiting that next breath. His mind simply cannot conceive of life without it, and panic sets in. This panic drives all his behavior. It is a horrible, terrifying situation in which to find oneself.

Added to all of this are the times of clarity when the addict sees that his situation has become desperate. He wants to quit, and he might make a solemn vow to never use again, only to pick it back up again a month, a week, a day or even an hour later. It is tempting to believe that he was lying all along, but he was not. He wanted to quit. He had every intention of quitting. But he suffers from a condition in which his own mind is working against him. His brain has become accustomed to the chemical, and it craves more. It will use every form of deception and trickery to move him into a position where he will use again. It will flood the body with physical cravings. It will lead him into situations where the drug will "accidentally" be encountered. He will visit old friends who are still using, placing himself directly in harm's way fully believing that he will not use. His mind tells him that he has control of this, that he can handle this, and he believes it. Someone might warn him about how dangerous it is to place himself in such a position, that he is likely to relapse if he does so.

But he will not believe it. His brain wants the drug and it will act outside of his own awareness, driving him ever onward toward relapse.

This is what makes it so hard for him to quit using. There is a saying, "Quitting is easy; it's not starting again that is hard." For an addict to stay off of drugs, he must stop trusting his own mind. This is harder than one might imagine. People who suffer from paranoid delusions are in a similar situation where their own thinking is causing them to fear imagined conspiracies. As long as they trust what their minds tell them, they cannot get better. But try telling a person suffering from paranoia that you are not a participant in the conspiracy he believes you to be a part of. Such a person will likely trust his mind absolutely, and he will believe your attempts to convince him otherwise are part of the plot against him. The addict suffers from a mind that is just this twisted, just this sick, and he is unaware of it. He will trust his thinking, and that thinking will lead him right back to the drug.

This is what my life had quickly become, and along with this insanity came the total breakdown in thinking that survival in this world requires. Cause and effect were no longer directly correlated in my mind. The idea that Cause X would result in Effect Y still existed. But along with it, the idea that Cause X was in no way related to Effect Y also possessed me. The sane thought was locked in battle with the insane thought, and the drug continued to fuel the insane one. I was lost in the middle, disconnected from it all.

I tell you this because the next stage of my journey will seem unthinkable to any sane mind. It is unthinkable to me now, and it is difficult for me to imagine how it was that I went there, even though I know that I did. I reached a point where I could play Russian Roulette with a fully loaded gun and somehow thought I could win. I know now that this is absurd, and I wish I could tell you I was blind to the absurdity of it then, but I wasn't. I knew it was absurd; but that knowledge did not carry with it sufficient force to limit my behavior.

Here is where my thinking led me. One, I still have money. Two, I will need more money to pay my bills and continue to support my drug habit. Three, if I buy meth in large enough quantities, I can sell it at an incredible profit. Four, my new "friends" will help me do this. Five, these friends will appreciate the fact that I can help them earn money and will therefore behave honorably. Six, I can continue this indefinitely and all will be well.

There is a certain logic to this kind of insane thinking. It requires an incredible amount of rationalization and denial, but a mind hell-bent on making sense of it can twist itself into doing so. My mind made sense of this quite well. It became, in my drug-fueled brain, the supremely rational road to happiness-ever-after. I truly believed this plan would solve all my problems, and life would be wonderful indeed.

And so I learned the mathematics of drug dealing. I could buy an ounce of meth for $600.00. An ounce of meth can be divided into 28 grams. Each gram could be sold for $50.00. That meant I could make $1,400.00 on my $600.00 investment, a profit of $800.00. I could take $1,200.00 from that to buy two more ounces and have two-hundred dollars left over for my personal use. A person could get rich quickly that way, and that was what I thought would happen to me.

Well, that was not what happened to me. I soon learned that it takes time to sell 28 grams of dope. In fact, it can take two or three days to sell it one gram at a time. I also learned that when you have dope, your "friends" are always trying to steal it from you. I fronted dope to people who never paid me as they promised. And I was continually smoking away whatever profits I imagined would make. I was lucky to break even and have my original $600.00 with which to purchase the next ounce.

It was then that Spider informed me that I could do better if I bought larger quantities. I could spend $5,000.00 on a pound, sell it by the ounce for $10,000.00 and make a larger profit in less time. People who buy ounces, he assured me, were more reliable, and were always seeking a steady source of good dope. It never occurred to me that people who bought ounces were idiots just like me struggling desperately to support their habit. No, this plan seemed to be the solution to all my problems, and it had the added benefit of supporting my contention that my original plan was a sound one; I was just thinking too small.

This is another strange reality of addiction. The mind believes the absurd idea that the solution to the problems associated with insane behavior, is the application of even more insane behavior. My mind now wrapped itself comfortably around the idea that supremely insane behavior was the ultimate solution to the problems mounting in my life. It was like getting burned while playing with fire. The drug-free mind would quickly learn that playing with fire was a bad thing and would therefore stop. The drug-fueled mind was able to convince itself that the problem was the fire was too small. An inferno was now in order.

So Spider introduced me to a man named Chuy. Chuy was said to be a member of the Mexican Mafia, and he had connections with gangs that moved large quantities of meth. This intrigued me. Infernos are like that. They have a fascinating allure that draws you in. You watch mesmerized by the destructiveness of it all.

Chuy came to my house with Spider and sat in my living room to talk. He was a Mexican man, about thirty years of age, with medium-length, jet-black hair and a small mustache. He was soft-spoken, and he tried his best to act like a real-life gangster. He seemed to me to be more a caricature of a gangster, but then, what did I know about gangsters?

Chuy explained to me that I could not be there on the first deal. The people he was purchasing the drugs from did not want to meet me until I had proven myself. If all went well on this first deal, I would be introduced to them the next time. He and Spider would take the money, make the deal, then bring me the meth. I told him that if this went well, there would be more business in the future and that we could all make a lot of money. So I gave Spider the money, my car to go make the deal, and my 9mm pistol in case anything went wrong. It all made perfect sense to me, and once again I thought I was on my way to a happy life in the drug game.

I learned that day that con men do not think long term. They think only in the here and now, and $5,000.00, my car and my gun was a big haul in the here and now. An hour later, when they still had not returned, I began calling their cell phones. Neither answered. I had been robbed and I knew it. I was livid, but there was nothing I could do about it. Then I received a phone call from Cindy.

Cindy was a woman I didn't really know. She was a Mexican woman in her mid-thirties and about the only thing I knew about her was that she sold meth. We met once in passing and said nothing but hello to one another. Then a strange thing happened. I began to receive phone calls from people threatening me that if I did anything to Cindy, they would kill me. It seems that someone overheard Spider's girlfriend, Nichole, saying that she and "Charles" were planning to kill Cindy and steal her dope and her money. Since Nichole was hanging around my place, everyone assumed this "Charles" to be me. Thus, the phone calls telling me to back off.

I assured everyone that I had no such plans and I went to Nichole to ask about it. She had no idea what these people were talking about, so I assumed the rumor was just started by some stupid tweaker who had nothing better to do. The event quickly blew over, but needless to say, Cindy wanted nothing to do with me.

It was because of all of that, I was surprised when she called me that evening. "Have you heard from Spider and Chuy?" she asked.

"No," I answered. "They ran off with my money and my car and I've not heard from them. They were supposed to pick up a package for me but they disappeared."

"I know," she said. "They are supposed to be getting that package from me."

I was shocked. I realized Chuy was nothing but a wannabe gangster connected to no one. Cindy was his girlfriend, and she was the one with the connections. I never really understood why she called me that night. She thought I wanted to kill her, and now she was telling me that her boyfriend and Spider were going to rob me. She knew where they were supposed to be meeting her and asked if I wanted to tag along. I told her I did, and she told me where to meet her. I grabbed my .38 revolver and went to meet Cindy in the parking lot of a convenience store. I jumped into the passenger seat of her black Camero, and off we went to meet Spider and Chuy.

We pulled into an apartment complex parking lot and there was my car. Cindy pulled behind them blocking them in. "Wait here," Cindy said as she stepped out of the car. Spider was in the driver's seat of my car and Chuy was in the passenger seat, facing away from us as we were behind them. I thought it strange that only Spider got out of the car; Chuy stayed seated, facing forward, not even looking back to see what was going on. I thought to myself that something was terribly wrong. Cindy was Chuy's girlfriend. Why did he stay in the car? Why wasn't he getting out to say hello? My body went on full alert, palms sweating, skin tingling. I looked over toward Spider and saw him fast approaching Cindy, his hand reaching toward the waistband of his pants where I had seen him place my 9mm pistol earlier that evening.

I cannot tell you what came over me in that instant. I didn't think, I simply acted. I jumped out of the car, .38 in hand.

"Back the fuck up, mother fucker!" I screamed. I was acting on pure meth-fueled adrenaline now. I was a wild animal and my eyes burned with fire. I saw Spider pause, his mind locked for a moment because he was shocked to see me. This gave me the one second delay I needed to get the drop on him. I had my .38 pointed at his head.

"Do anything stupid and I will fucking kill you," I shouted. I moved toward him, reached into the waistband of his pants and retrieved my 9mm. Chuy then jumped out of the car.

"Stop right there, you piece of shit!" I ordered, and I found myself holding two guns pointed at the two men.

"Give me my fucking money," I shouted. Spider complied. He reached into his pocket, retrieved the money and handed it to me. I was in a hurry now. I was in an apartment complex parking lot in the middle of the night, guns drawn, shouting orders. The police were sure to be coming soon. I had to get out of there.

"You two get the fuck out of here and don't come back," I screamed, and they went running off into the night. I jumped in my car, Cindy jumped into hers, and we both took off.

I later learned that Spider's real name was Charles. A guy named Charles *was* planning to kill Cindy and take her dope and money. It just wasn't *me*. The plan was to put out the rumor of Nichole and me doing the killing, killing Cindy with my gun, then, he and Chuy would disappear, leaving me and Nichole to take the blame. The strange thing about all this was that Cindy called me to go with her that night. The very person she once thought was planning to kill her actually saved her life. Had I not been there she would have died. It was a strange coincidence to be sure. It would not be the last.

For any normal person, this would have been more than enough to say, "That's it, I quit." But that is the point, isn't it? I was no longer a normal person; I was an addict. This was not danger to be avoided; this was instead some exhilarating shit. This was life lived as I never dreamed it could be lived. This was excitement. I handled my business like a man and was proud of it. I was pushing life to the very edge, and I could do so because I no longer cared whether I lived or died.

I had wandered too close to the event horizon of the black hole of drug addiction, and I was now in the area from which there would be no escape. The gravity of a black hole is so strong that light cannot escape from it. It is life that cannot escape from the gravity of addiction.

By now I was completely out of control. My life seemed to be nothing but fun and excitement, but clearly, in retrospect, it wasn't really fun at all. My drug-stimulated mind led me to believe that this was life lived to the fullest—life pushed to the very edge. But something was missing. Deep inside of me there developed a blackness in the pit of my soul. This blackness was growing and was beginning to consume me. It was a void that no amount of excitement, no amount of drugs, no amount of anything could ever fill. But this fact eluded me. This darkness cried out constantly demanding that it be fed. More of anything seemed to calm it, at least for a moment. But inevitably it would awaken, craving more. Soon the only thing that would quiet it was the drug, and that never lasted long.

This was the trap. I had become a slave to this thing I had come to know as my self. My every waking moment was spent in service to its wants, its needs, its desires. I was no longer running the show; it was. And whatever I did for it was never enough. *It* always demanded more. *It* felt like a monster pursuing me, threatening at any moment to swallow me whole. The darkness was forever nipping at my heels, and I ran desperately, in a vain attempt to stay one step ahead. The terror and desperation that hovered at the fringe of my awareness had become my constant companion. And my drug-fueled sense of denial kept me convinced that somehow I could manage, somehow I could keep it from falling apart. I could not.

Looking back, I am overwhelmed with the sense that life has some strange intelligence to it. It seems as if every event in my life occurred so as to bring me toward some mystical revelation. Life was trying to teach me something, and I did not want to learn. I was locked in a battle with life, and I was struggling to win, using every means at my disposal to do so. But life is also patient. All of the energy I put into fighting against it only served to strengthen its resolve. I know now that this was a battle I could not win. But at the time, I was not yet ready to give up.

Charles Bynum

CHAPTER SIX

That which does not kill us makes us stronger. – Friedrich Nietzsche

I was running full speed now toward certain doom, and yet, I felt as if I was on top of the world. Cindy had become my connection to a steady and regular supply of dope. I had people regularly buying from me and was beginning to make money. Everyone loved me because I was the guy with the drugs. I once heard a preacher say that sin will take you farther than you ever wanted to go, will keep you longer than you ever wanted to stay, and will cost you more than you ever wanted to pay. It is a funny thing about being on top of the world—you tend to fall off the other side.

I was at a friend's house one evening, partying into the late hours and decided I was tired and wanted to go home. It was about 1:30 in the morning when I arrived home. I had grown tired of all the people, of all the incessant chatter and wanted to be alone. So it was that I was alone that night.

At about two in the morning, I heard a noise in the house. I went to my dresser and retrieved a knife that I kept there. I opened my bedroom door to investigate and there stood four men. Two I immediately recognized as "friends" who bought dope from me. The other two I had never seen before. They were all big, bad, mean and ugly. Time slowed to a near standstill. My mind raced. In the space of less than one second, I had time to think to myself that these men were here to do me harm, that I was trapped with nowhere to run, nowhere to hide, and that my only hope was to attack them first.

I lunged forward, knife in hand, determined to attack the biggest of the four. I swung my knife at him, attempting to stab him in the belly, but the man standing next to him hit my arm and the knife missed its mark, hitting his thigh instead. I then swung the knife at the guy who made me miss, cutting a gash in his hand. I learned that night that when four men attack you, they don't do it like they do in the movies. In the movies, they have the decency to come at you one at a time. In real life, however, you find eight fists flying toward your face all at once. And to my great chagrin, all eight immediately landed, knocking me straight onto my back. As big and bad as my drug-fueled mind believed myself to be, I only lasted about two seconds in that fight.

They held me down and took my knife from me. I remembered thinking that, at any moment, I would feel the cold blade of my own knife as it was thrust in me, but that did not happen. The men took a nearby electrical cord and tied my feet and hands behind my back. I was lying, face down, hog tied, when they started beating me. Two men were on either side of me beating me in the face. No matter which way I turned, I found another fist slamming violently into me. The other two men were kicking me repeatedly in my sides. I thought to myself, "This is it. This is how I am going to die." Eventually the men took a break to ransack my home to look for drugs, money and anything of value they could steal. Then they came back to beat me some more. This continued for what seemed an eternity, until, at long last, darkness descended upon me.

I awoke some time later, choking, unable to breathe. I soon realized that the puddle of blood that had pooled under my head was so deep that I was breathing it in. I turned my head to the side so I could inhale air instead of blood. I managed to work my hands free, and with great difficulty, rolled myself onto my side. I knew I had to get up, but the pain was so great, I could barely move. I laid there for some time, summoning my strength. "You have to get up," I told myself. "You have to move."

I gritted my teeth and forced my body to comply. I moaned in agony as I slowly lifted myself from the floor. When I could finally stand, I saw the horror of it all.

There was a huge puddle of blood in the carpet where my head had been. Blood spatter covered the walls. It looked as if a brutal murder had taken place, and I had no doubt that murder was what those men intended. I remembered that a human body contains approximately seven liters of blood. I was looking at what appeared to be seven gallons. I thought I should be dead; surely no one could survive such a massive blood loss. I staggered into the bathroom and saw my face beaten and swollen beyond recognition. I cleaned my wounds as best I could with arms that could barely move because my ribs were broken. I thought about calling for help, about getting to a hospital, but I could not risk doing either. The police would be called, my home searched and they might find drugs.

I decided I had to leave. I was afraid to stay in my home, thinking the men who did this to me might return. They took my cell phone and, as I had no land line, I could not call anyone to come over. I pulled myself together as best I could, got into my car, and drove across town to my friend Ed's house. Ed was someone I regularly got high with, and I thought he could help me. It was about 3:30 in the morning when I knocked on his door. He opened it.

"I need help, Ed," I said, barely able to speak.

"Who are you?" he asked, and I realized that I had been beaten so badly, he didn't even recognize me.

"It's me, Charles," I said.

"Oh my God!" he exclaimed. "Get in here." Ed took me by the arm and led me to his sofa, where I sat down. "What happened to you?" he asked.

I told Ed what had happened then drifted off to sleep.

The next day, I borrowed Ed's phone and called Heather to come take me home. She helped me into bed, and over the following couple of days, nursed me back to health. She cleaned up the blood as best she could, but my home was forever stained with the event of that night. Heather found my cell phone. The men had not taken it, but threw it aside so I was unable to find it. And what did I do? I called Cindy and asked her to bring me some more dope so I could start the insanity all over again. But things would never be the same. It was no longer fun. It was now a trap from which I was unable to escape. I wanted out, but I did not know how to get out.

At this point I was confronted with the true horror of my addiction. The men that came to my home that night meant to kill me. I knew that when they found out that I was still alive, they would be afraid that I would come kill them in retaliation. This meant that there was no doubt that they would be forced to come back and finish the job. In their twisted minds, they had to kill me or else I would kill them. It was not true; I did not want to kill them nor would I have done so. But they did not know this and they were certain to assume otherwise. This meant that I *had* to kill them, because if I didn't, they would surely kill me.

This was the horror. I am not a killer, but I felt that I had to kill in order to survive. The only other alternative I could think of was to quickly sell enough dope to make enough money so I could leave town. And I had to hope that I could do this before they realized that I was still alive and came to kill me. I found myself trapped in a nightmare from which I could not escape, and the stakes were nothing short of life and death.

So that was what I did. I began selling dope as fast as I could, as cheaply as I could, so that I could get out as soon as I could. The insanity of my addiction had dissolved into sheer desperation. I, a successful, educated man, had been reduced to this.

Charles Bynum

CHAPTER SEVEN

How much more grievous are the consequences of anger than the causes of it. – Marcus Aurelius

I then learned an important lesson about dealing drugs: Doing so brings a steady stream of traffic to your home both night and day. People show up to buy dope, then leave, one after another, day after day. This activity quickly attracted the attention of the police. And before I knew it they came knocking at my door. Only they didn't come knocking like normal people do; they came knocking with battering rams.

Early one morning they came in force. It is all just a blur now—pandemonium and panic, guns flashing, shouting of orders, terror. It was the sense that my world, and everything in it, just exploded. My world did explode that day, and life would never be the same.

And so I awoke one day and found myself in prison. It is a funny thing to find yourself in such a situation. The drug that promised me so much now abandoned me completely. It led me down a path to utter destruction, and now that it delivered me there, it no longer had any use for me. Another funny thing happened. After a few days, the effects of the drug left me, and I found myself becoming more like the person I once was. It was like falling asleep, moving into some crazy dream, then awakening to find it was not a dream after all, it was real, and now I was the one left to pay for all that had transpired. It was one big lie. The demon meth promised so much and delivered so little.

The first thing I noticed about prison was that my world shrank. Everything was small, contained. I lived in a small space, and was sometimes allowed out of that small space to wander about in a larger small space. During certain times prisoners are allowed outside in the yard, which is nothing but an outdoor small space. Where I once had the world at my disposal to wander about in, I now had an area about one-hundred yards square in which to live out my entire existence. The sense of confinement weighed heavily upon me, crushing me so completely that even the air seemed heavier when I breathed.

The second thing I noticed about prison was the incredible sense of boredom. People who have not been to prison think the first thing you would notice is the terror born of the danger that lurks everywhere. But no. The danger and terror come later. Boredom is the real nemesis for those who are incarcerated. And boredom carries with it its own set of problems. I had spent every minute of my waking life in an attempt to avoid any confrontation with myself. And now I was left for hour after hour with nothing but the very self I had sought to avoid. This is the true torment of prison. There were no distractions. There was just me and my suffering. And with no distractions, that suffering soon burned white hot.

The third thing I noticed about prison was that life no longer required that I make any decisions. Every decision was made for me. 5:30AM, an obnoxious buzzer sounds as the inhuman florescent lights flicker to life, alerting the prisoner that it is time for standing count. We groggily stand beside our bunks for the fifteen minutes or so it takes for the prisoners to be counted. 6:00AM, the buzzer sounds again, and the cell door opens signaling chow time. We march single file around the yard to the chow hall and eat the utter garbage they call food. 6:30 AM, a buzzer sounds in the chow hall alerting us that it is time to march back to the housing unit. Then we had what was called "free time" in which we could wander about in the day hall of the housing unit. Some prisoners play cards, some play chess, others simply visit. 10:00AM, the buzzer sounds for yard time. We file out into the yard where we can work out on the weight pile, or wander aimlessly in a circle around the yard. 11:00, buzzer sounds, time to return to the cell for afternoon count. 11:30, buzzer sounds signaling chow time, and again, we march to the chow hall. 12:00, buzzer, time to return to the housing unit. 3:00, buzzer, yard time again. 4:00, buzzer, return to cell for evening count. 4:30, buzzer, time for chow. 5:00, buzzer, return to housing unit. 8:00, buzzer, return to cell for night count. 9:00, buzzer, lights out.

This is what life becomes; this is what my life had become. Life lived at the beck and call of a buzzer. Day after day, week after week, month after month, year after year, always the same routine. Time slows until you think it has completely stood still. Incessant, relentless monotony is the order of the day, every day. There is nothing like it. And some men cannot take it. They simply go mad.

The new men to prison are referred to as "fish" by those who have been in for some time. What is not said is that those who have been in for awhile have become "sharks." New prisoners are fish swimming amongst sharks, and are therefore shark food. Like any small fish, survival depends upon the ability to blend in, to exist unnoticed. Do that well, and a fish just might be fortunate enough to grow into a shark itself one day. Make any mistake, and a horrifically violent death is certain.

So how does one exist unnoticed in such a confined space filled with hundreds of men? The first thing I did was force myself to become intensely aware of everything around me. I was now living in close proximity to some of the most evil people to ever walk the planet. Murderers and rapists abounded. Violence could erupt at any moment without warning, without provocation. So I learned to remain ever alert to the possibility of danger. This was where the boredom of prison could get me. Everything became so routine that I was soon tempted to let down my guard. It takes a great deal of energy to exist in a constant state of vigilance, and my body fought against this. It longed to relax into the routine. It desired the illusion of safety, and boredom and routine can present the illusion of safety. This was a mistake that could get me killed. I told myself that I must always watch for every possibility. The man who I think to be my friend walks up to me smiling, like he is happy to see me. What I don't know is that he is hiding a shank he intends to stick in my neck. Something about his demeanor *will* give him away, but I must be alert, I must be aware of everything, or else I will miss it. I could not afford to try to make sense of it; that was itself a distraction that would cost me the precious second or two that I would otherwise have in which to save myself. Trying to make sense of it serves no purpose. I learned I must deal with "what is," I was not afforded the luxury of dealing with "what should be." My "friend" may not have any issue with me at all. I may have inadvertently looked at someone else wrong, that man took offense and he has now hired or coerced my "friend" into killing me. *Why* things were happening did not matter. *That* things were happening is what I had to deal with. I could not allow my mind to go into the why. No one was really my friend. Everyone was out to do the same thing I was out to do—survive. And there were a few who wanted nothing more than to inflict senseless violence upon whomever they could. My only option was to adjust, or die.

My cellie was a man named Ray. "Cellie" is a prison term meaning cell mate. I learned many such terms. Prison has a language all its own. "Big Ray" they called him; I assumed he got the name because he was so small. He appeared to be about fifty years old. I later learned he was seventy-three. He was on his bunk when I first carried my bedroll into the cell. He was reading a book as I entered. He looked up at me. "I'll give you a minute to get situated," he said dryly as he closed his book and stood to leave the cell. He was watching me intently as he left the cell, sizing me up. He and I were going to spend much time together in a very small space, and he was taking in everything about me. There was something very animal-like in the encounter. I was sizing him up too, but this was unlike anything I had done in the real world. Something about the danger of prison made me learn to listen to my body. And my body spoke to me more clearly than my mind ever did. It does not rationalize like my mind does. It simply senses. My mind, if I were to let it, would take what my body senses and try to turn it into something amenable to me, something safe and comfortable. I simply could not allow that. I had to listen to my body exactly as it presented the situation.

Having said that, I must now say that the mind plays an important role here as well. For it is the mind that formulates a response to what the body is telling it. There is a delicate balance to be attained here. Men in prison tend to be the type who are completely ruled by their physiological responses, devoid of a mind to guide them. They are slaves to their emotions. Their body speaks, they instantly react, no thought, no deliberation. It is a very primal, very animal existence—inhuman. Everything is seen short-term; most inmates have no concept of long-term consequences. The trick is to allow the mind to analyze what the body is telling it without adding or taking anything away. Perception is the process of taking sensory input from the body, then constructing a reality colored by your own experiences and fears. What I had to learn in prison was to take that sensory input and see it as it was, without any coloring from the mind. My body was telling me that Ray was not too much of a threat; that we just might get along. It was best to go along with that, while remaining aware that my mind might, and I must stress the word "might", be coloring this situation in such a way as to delude me into a false sense of security. I would go with what my body was telling me, while remaining open to any new data that might later present itself. Nothing was concrete. Nothing was decided. Today Ray was not a threat. Tomorrow he might become a threat. Everything must remain fluid in just this way. This was not easy to do. My mind wanted to place everyone into neat little categories—friend or foe—then leave them there. To do so is to abandon the "what is" in favor of the "what I want my world to be." I could get killed in the "what is" because I was blinded by the "what I want my world to be." Prison is about seeing what is, exactly *as it is*.

Ray walked out into the day hall and I began unpacking the few belongings the prison had issued to me. I unrolled my two-inch thick piece of tattered padding they called a mattress onto my steel bunk. I placed my clothing and the small towel they gave me into a drawer that slid out from under my bunk. That was it, I had moved in to my new home. I hopped onto my bunk and began to reassure myself that I would be okay, that I could do this. Not that I really believed it, but I needed to try to convince myself anyway. I had learned much during my time in county jail awaiting transport to prison. If I kept to myself, minded my own business, perhaps I could survive this. I was terrified, but I could not allow that fear to control me. I had to breathe through it. I had to learn to make it a part of me, as opposed to allowing *me* to become a part of *it*.

Now at this point I really must speak about God. I've heard soldiers say that there are no atheists on a battlefield. I think the same concept applies to prison. I found myself feeling a strong desire to turn to God for support, and this irritated me. I had some vague concept of God, but it was an ephemeral concept at best. God was certainly not a presence in my life, and I doubted such a thing really existed. Even if he did exist, I hated him. Life had been very unfair to me and I could see no God in any of it. I certainly wanted nothing to do with a God who could have allowed such horrors to happen to me. To my way of thinking, the entire idea seemed silly and weak. People invented God as a psychological crutch to carry them through difficult times. Fear drove them to construct a concept of some all-caring, all loving being that would care for and comfort them. I had no desire to seek comfort in an illusion.

Yet here I was, longing to turn to God. I was alone in an alien world fraught with danger and uncertainty, and my mind, just like the mind of every religious zealot I had ever known, now wanted to construct an illusion with which I could comfort myself. I wondered about this as I lay on my bunk. I felt split in two. I longed for it at the same time I fought against it. What I did not realize at the time was that it was not my mind longing for God at all. My mind was actually fighting against it, telling me how foolish, how silly and how simple-minded such a thing was. The longing in me was actually coming from somewhere else. I mentioned before that in prison you learn to listen to your body. It was because I *was* listening to my body that I was becoming aware of this urge toward the divine. It was my physical being that was longing for God, not my mind. But at this point, my mind was too firmly in control for me to recognize this.

Ray came back into the cell, laid down on his bunk and began to read. He said nothing, and I knew not to say anything myself. Prison is about respect, but I must be very careful in my use of words if I am to be understood. Respect does not mean the same thing in prison that it means in the real world. Because of this, when I say prison is about respect, I am saying one thing, and you are likely hearing another. In the real world, respect is something earned. You are afforded respect because you behave in a manner worthy of respect. In prison, respect is something *demanded*. It is a word that carries with it an unspoken code of conduct that you must adhere to or you risk violent reprisal. In the real world, respect is conferred upon you due to your fair and kind treatment of others. In prison, respect is something you inflict on others through your willingness to react violently toward anyone who fails to give it to you. It is not the same thing even though it is the same word

Since I was the one moving into Ray's home, respect meant that I allow him to be the first to speak. But my silence also served to assert my demand that he respect me. I was not catering to him and trying to win him over as a friend. I was not going to be his little bitch and attempt to kiss his ass. To do that would be to betray weakness and fear. If he wanted to be quiet, I could be quiet too. My silence told him many things. It said, "I don't need you. I am fine on my own." It also said, "I respect your desire not to talk to me. I will afford you your space." And it said that I understood the basic rules even though I was a fish. Yes, Ray and I were carrying on an entire conversation with one another, even though no words were being spoken.

About an hour passed before Ray laid down his book, looked over to me, and spoke. "What's your name?" he asked.

"Charles," I answered.

"First time?"

"Yes."

"Then I want you to understand a couple simple rules," he said. "The fact that you are living in this cell with me does not mean that I am your friend. I didn't choose you, and you didn't choose me. So don't look for me to back you on anything. This is a small space. Keep things clean and tidy and we'll get along just fine. Understood?"

"Understood," I replied. And that was the extent of my first conversation with Ray.

CHAPTER EIGHT

All religions must be tolerated…for every man must get to heaven in his own way. – Epictetus

Not long after I arrived in prison I witnessed my first stabbing. We were walking to the chow hall when someone came running up behind me and bumped me with his shoulder as he rushed by. A moment of terror surged through me as my mind wandered in that surreal area that exists between the event and awareness of the event. The next thing I knew, I saw a shank buried into the neck of the man walking in front of me. He fell to the ground, blood spurting in a heartbeat rhythm. My instinctive reaction was to lend assistance to the dying man, and I found myself moving toward him. I suddenly felt the powerful hand of another prisoner grabbing the back of my shirt. "Step over him and just keep on moving," the man said. "This is none of your business." The man forcefully moved me forward, and I complied.

I learned in that moment that to render assistance was to invite trouble. To render aid would mean to take a side, thereby resulting in this man's enemies becoming my own. The yard alarm sounded with a noise like an air raid siren, signaling everyone to drop face-first onto the ground. Guards came running from everywhere, and I also learned that rendering assistance can be mistaken for an attack, and that will get you shot by the tower guards. It was an upside down world in which the most basic human kindness would get you killed. This is the not-so-subtle way in which prison began its insidious transformation, bleeding everything human from my soul.

I felt sick, and I felt a growing fear that my environment was truly one of constant danger. I was also surprised by the fact that I could become so calloused as to step over a man bleeding to death beneath me and feel so detached from it all. My body distanced me from the horror of it as best it could, but I paid the price of nausea. I hated it here. I wondered how I would survive this place.

"You're going to have to relax into this or it will drive you insane," Ray told me one night after lockdown.

"Relax into it?" I thought, though I said nothing. I wondered what he meant. Ray had a quiet calmness to him even in the midst of all this madness. He seemed to be at ease no matter what was going on around him. Nothing seemed to rattle him and he never seemed to take anything personally. I could not quite put my finger on it, but I felt a sense of peace when he was around. This was a good thing I suppose, because the two of us were forced into spending a lot of time together.

"You won't be able to think your way through this," he continued. Ray had not been one to talk much, so this comment was unusual for him.

"What do you mean?" I asked.

"You are living in a crazy world, my friend…" I noticed he said, "My friend." He had never said such a thing to me before. Those words were his subtle prison way of telling me that I had gained a degree of acceptance with him. "You will never be able to make sense of this place so you may as well stop trying," he continued. "Trying to make sense of this place will bring you up into your head. That's where you are right now. That's why you're so tense. I can feel it coming off of you."

I had no idea what he was talking about.

"You have to let it all go now," he added.

"Let what go?" I asked.

"Everything that ever defined who you think you are. You must let go of your past. Your past cannot help you in here. Nothing you ever learned from your past will be of any benefit to you. You also have to let go of the future. Thinking about how things will one day be is dangerous."

"I don't understand," I said weakly.

"You are trying to make sense of this place based on everything you learned in the past. But this place is not like anything you've ever experienced before. Your past will cripple you here. You will expect things to happen based on how they happened out in the real world. This will blind you to how things are actually happening now."

I thought about this for a moment. "So you're saying the rules are different in here?"

"There you go," Ray replied. "I said nothing about rules. Rules are one of those things from your past that you are trying to apply in here. You're thinking that all you need to do is modify what you think the rules are, and suddenly all will be well. I'm saying let go of even the *idea* of rules. Your belief in rules will get you hurt the minute you run into someone who has no interest in what you believe the rules to be."

"I understand that people won't always live by my idea of the rules," I answered. "But I can figure out what their rules are and then predict what they will do."

"You can't predict a fucking thing," Ray snapped. "You start predicting what you think is going to happen and you won't see what *is* happening right in front of you. That's what I'm trying to tell you. You're using the past to try to predict the future, and because of that, you are unable to see what is happening right here and right now. You're in your head. You best get yourself fully in this world, and you best do it now."

"But I am in this world right here *and* right now," I insisted. "Where else do you think I could be?" Ray was getting irritated with me. He was trying to tell me something, and I just wasn't getting it.

"There are two ways to learn things in this world, partner—the easy way, or the hard way. I'm trying to tell you the easy way. You can bet that if you don't catch on, life will start teaching you the hard way."

"I'm listening to you. I'm just not sure what you're trying to say. I mean, I'm always paying attention to everything. I just don't understand…"

"You're paying attention to the wrong thing," Ray interrupted. "You're seeing what's in your head, not what is." He took in a deep breath and slowly exhaled. "Listen," he continued. "What's in your head is words. Words are not reality. They are instead you describing to yourself what is happening around you. It's a constant dialog in which you are saying to yourself, this is happening now, this is what it means, this is what I need to do to prepare myself. All of that chatter is slowing you down, getting in the way of your ability to see things as they are. You need to let all of that go. Start observing what is going on around you *without* your mental dialog."

I stared blankly at Ray. I had no idea what he was talking about. I tried to speak. My mouth moved about in a vain attempt to form words but nothing issued forth. Ray shook his head in exasperation. "That's okay," he said. "You'll see it soon enough, I suppose."

Ray rolled over and went to sleep. He was irritated with me, yet I couldn't shake the feeling that he was trying to warn me about something, trying to help me in some way. I just didn't know how. I started to think old Ray was a bit touched in the head, but then, he had survived twenty years in this place and seemed to have done so reasonably well. I could not simply dismiss his words. I lay awake in my bunk for many hours that night trying to make sense of what Ray had said. I was overcome by an uneasy feeling that something bad was about to happen, and that Ray somehow knew what it was.

• • •

"Do you have a personal relationship with Jesus?"

I was in the prison chaplain's office. One of the inmates had invited me to attend the Sunday morning services, and I was not certain why I agreed to go. I suppose boredom was the primary motivator. It was an excuse to do something other than the standard nothing. After the sermon I was introduced to the chaplain, and before I knew what happened, I found myself sitting in his office for what I knew would be his attempt to save my poor lost soul. It was irritating and entertaining at the same time.

"I'm not sure I know what you mean," I replied.

"Jesus loves you, my friend," the chaplain continued. "God sent him to die on the cross for our sins."

I stared blankly at the man. I've never been particularly fond of Christians. There was something about Christianity that struck me as disingenuous. That's not exactly right. There was something about *Christians* that struck me as disingenuous. Christianity was, I thought, misguided. It was just too external for my liking. The idea that someone or something else was going to save me, never sat well with me. It seemed lazy, weak.

"If you will accept Jesus as your personal savior, your life will turn around and you will never have to worry again about spending an eternity suffering in Hell," he said to me.

I would like to say that Jesus descended from a cloud and saved my sorry, sinful self that day. God knows I've read many such stories while in prison because most of the books in the prison library are donated by various churches. But that was not to be my path. No, Jesus coming to save me like some mystical superhero was too easy. I knew this, of course, but the preacher didn't know it yet. He was about to find out.

"I'm not too worried about Hell, preacher," I said.

A concerned look came over him. "The Bible says that we will burn in Hell unless we give our lives to Christ," he said. "Jesus is the one and only path to God."

"I think the stories in the Bible are mostly metaphor," I replied. Big mistake. His eyes grew wide in disbelief. I might as well have said that I just raped his mother.

"I believe in a literal interpretation of the Bible," he said, the smile on his face wound just a bit too tightly, betraying his hidden contempt for me. "God's word is written here in black and white, and I believe it as God wrote it."

At this point, my mind raced with thoughts of things I would *like* to say but knew would be utterly useless *to* say. My first thought was that his phrase "literal interpretation" was an oxymoron. To interpret something is to come to a subjective understanding or explanation. It is a personal interaction with the written word. How one can do that "literally" is beyond me. No two people ever read the same words the same. Words don't actually speak to you, they interact with you, drawing their power and meaning from your own personal experiences—experiences that are uniquely yours. When people speak of a literal interpretation, what they really mean is an interpretation that is objective, universally applicable to all. But "objective" is a funny little word that has a definition and yet contains no meaning. Nothing is objective. I can only experience life as me, and that experience is completely subjective. Everyone experiences everything subjectively. We consider something to be objective when an arbitrarily determined number of subjective opinions agree. That is absurd.

So before me sat a preacher speaking of a literal interpretation of the Bible. What he really meant was that he and his cohorts agreed on a particular *subjective* interpretation. They then determined this subjective interpretation to be objective by virtue of their agreement. Next, they labeled this so-called objective interpretation literal. It was nothing but a trick of the mind designed to impose upon reality whatever it was they wanted to force the world into believing. I knew all of this, but the situation that was presenting itself to me precluded me from giving voice to these thoughts. You simply cannot argue with stupidity, and stupidity reinforced by a closed mind is an impenetrable wall. What sat before me now was stupidity reinforced by a closed mind in the form of this preacher.

The next thought that came to mind was how uninterested this preacher was in me. Oh, he professed to be concerned for my immortal soul for sure, but was he really? He never asked about me, my experiences or my beliefs because I was not a human being to him. I was a project. He was not concerned for my soul; he was concerned about his role. This meant that he sought his identity through his belief that he was saving others. He was the anointed one, the keeper of God's truth. I was the lost sinner who needed that truth, whether or not I was aware of this fact. This was not a human interaction. This was an interaction between roles. He was to don one role, I was to don the other, and then we were to allow the roles to interact. It was like playing make-believe. And I was supposed to agree to the make-believe rules, the first of which was that his concern for the role interaction somehow meant he cared about me. This was actually the lie designed to lure me into participation. To imply this was being done out of concern for me was the coercion to trick me into compliance. I was supposed to engage this because he meant well and cared about me. Bullshit. That is like the fish saying the fisherman means well and cares about me because he put a worm on his hook. It was the old bait and switch technique. It was actually a battle of egos. My true purpose, in his mind, was to play the role of sinner in need of saving. He could then save me, with the inevitable result being that he could feel good about himself as his ego reveled in the fact that he was the personal messenger of God. It was a silly little game that did not interest me at all. It seemed a stupid waste of time.

All of these thoughts flooded my mind, and yet not one of them was worth voicing. I mean, what was really going to happen? Was I going to speak the magical combination of words that would bring this man to an understanding of the situation as I saw it? Was he going to come to some profound realization because of anything I might say? I think not. You cannot teach anything to a man who already knows everything. What you can do is toy with him, fuck with his reality a bit. That may sound a bit mean, or it may even seem a waste of time, but it had the overwhelming appeal of being entertaining. At that moment I felt I could use a bit of entertainment.

"So you want me to embrace this literal interpretation of the Bible, surrender, and let Jesus save me from Hell? It that it?" I asked.

"That's exactly it, my son," he replied, his voice softening as he began to fool himself into believing that I was succumbing to his manipulations. In his mind, he was now like Jesus. In my mind he was jacking off, and I was the porn he was doing it to.

"I have read the New Testament of the Bible, preacher," I said. "And I have always had a problem with the fact that the teachings of the church don't seem to be in accord with what Jesus taught." I was setting him up. I was playing into his expectations of me based on my awareness of the role he wanted me to play. I was acting as if I was going along with his little game and he fell right into it.

"We teach the same love Jesus taught," he said.

"When I read the Bible, I saw Jesus as a man who was sharing with others his spiritual experience. He never attempted to coerce others into believing anything. Instead, he took a personal interest in the suffering of others, listened to them, comforted them, and then showed them the respect of not trying to force them into anything. He didn't claim to know the one and only path. He stated his experience and then he allowed others to choose."

"Jesus was not a man, he was God made flesh," he stated sternly.

"So Jesus was God?"

"Exactly," the preacher answered.

"Then I don't understand something. In the Lord's Prayer, Jesus begins by saying 'Our Father who art in Heaven'."

"Yes."

"Shouldn't he have said instead, 'Me who art on Earth?'"

"Well, no," the preacher replied, his irritation growing. "He was giving an example of how to pray. He knew he was God, but he wanted to show others how to pray to God."

"So he was lying?" I asked.

"No, he wasn't lying."

"But I never read anything where he prefaced the prayer by saying something like, 'Although I am God, this is how to pray to me later when I'm gone,' or anything like that. He was praying as if he were a man."

There was a long pause, then the preacher said, "There are some mysteries of God that we human beings simply cannot understand."

I have always loved that one. People like this preacher attempt to convince you of the truth of their position with logic, and the minute logic fails them, they hide behind the "mysterious nature of God." It is beautifully circular logic, and it bails them out of any inconsistency. I knew this, but I decided to let that one slide.

"So Jesus is the son of God?" I asked.

"Yes, and he was sent to save your soul."

"And I am the son of God too, right?"

"Noooo…" he said as if I had wandered into the depths of Hell itself. "Jesus is the one and only son of God."

"But didn't I read somewhere when Jesus was asked if he was the son of God, he replied, 'Yes, and you are all my brother and my sisters?'"

"Well, yes…"

"That would mean we are all children of God just like him, right?"

"Well, no…"

"You said you believed in a literal interpretation of the Bible. These are Jesus' own words. Taken literally, he is telling me that I am the son of God too."

"Jesus said, 'No one gets to the Father but through me,'" the preacher protested.

"Well that sounds like a contradiction. How can I take the Bible literally if it contradicts itself?"

"There is no contradiction," he said. "Jesus is the one and only son of God. When he said, 'You are my brothers and my sisters,' what he meant was that God loves us all."

I paused to consider his words. "Ok," I said. "So I am not to take what Jesus said literally. I am instead to divine what he *really* meant as opposed to what he *actually* said?"

"Exactly," the preacher replied.

So much for literal interpretation, I thought. But I was even more amazed at how this preacher was completely unaware of his inconsistency. The mind is funny that way. It can gather its perceptions, and then arrange them so as to create any reality it wants. It simply ignores the absurdities, tosses them aside as if they never existed. It then convinces itself of the logical necessity of its absurd logic. To be fair, this is not unique to Christians. We all do this outside of our awareness. But this preacher *was* a Christian and this was what this Christian was doing at this moment. And I was venting my pent-up hostility toward him simply because he was presenting me the opportunity to do so and it pleased me. He was, to me, not a human being at all. He was a mind interacting with a reality he had created for himself out of nothing. You cannot argue with a mind, you can only react to it. Or you can ignore it. I chose to ignore it.

"Preacher," I said growing tired of this game, "I think Jesus was a man who had a spiritual revelation he attempted to share with others. I think that if he were to return to Earth today and see what is being taught in his name, he would be appalled. I think people are inherently lazy, so they began to worship him as God, when he attempted to open their eyes to the fact that God was already inside each and every one of them. I don't think Jesus wanted to save anyone. He wanted to show people that they could save themselves." This sounded good, though I doubt that even I believed any of it.

The preacher could not hide his disdain. "Well, I feel sorry for you then," he said, his words dripping with contempt. "An eternity in Hell awaits you."

He seemed to take comfort in his belief that I would burn in Hell, that this God who so loved me was sure to punish me for an eternity. I never understood that. I would think that such a realization would have broken his heart. After all, he loved me and wanted only to save my soul, right? The fact that I would be condemned to Hell should have instilled in him a sense of sorrow. But that was where the lie manifested. He was not concerned about me. In fact, he was quite pleased that I would be punished. After all, I was there to serve the needs of his ego, and I did not comply so I would now get what I deserved. I was no longer of any use to him, and he terminated the conversation.

I can't say why I engaged in such silly behavior that day. I suppose my anger *toward* God found its expression in the person of this man, who in my mind, was attempting to present himself as the representative *of* God. Or maybe I'm over thinking this. It could have been nothing more than boredom and anger. I was angry with the world, and angry with a God who would allow the misery I was now experiencing to exist. Or perhaps I just felt like being mean to someone who probably did not deserve to be treated in the manner in which I treated him. Who knows, and who cares? It was what it was, and I did what I did. The fact was that I just didn't care much about anything anymore. It was just a bunch of meaningless stuff happening. God, how I hated it all.

• • •

My conversation with the preacher became my obsession of the day. All I could think of was how much I hated him, how phony he was, what a hypocrite I thought him to be. Hate is like that. It will latch on to whatever is available at the moment. And I must admit there were times when it felt really good to hate. It tasted especially sweet when I had nothing else, so, hatred was the flavor I gave my life that day.

"So why are you so upset with the prison chaplain?" Ray asked later that night after lockdown.

"How did you know I was angry with the chaplain?" I asked.

Ray tilted his head and looked at me as if I was an idiot. "You've been bitching about him to anyone who will listen all day," he said.

"So you heard that?" I asked.

"Everyone heard it, Charles," he replied.

I thought it funny that he said this. I was not aware of the fact that I had been talking about it all day. But I had been. Ray must have overheard me because I had said nothing directly to him.

"That Chaplain just pisses me off," I said.

"Why?" Ray asked.

I thought about his question before answering. "It's just that I don't like Christians," I said.

"Why don't you like Christians, Charles," Ray replied.

"Because they are all hypocrites," I answered with a surge of anger welling up inside of me.

Ray was quiet for a moment. Then he spoke, "You're painting with a rather broad brush aren't you?"

"Here we go," I thought to myself. "What do you mean, Ray?" I asked, my voice betraying my irritation.

"You are saying that all Christians are as that preacher is," he said.

"So? It's true isn't it?"

"I don't know that," Ray answered. "I think that there is truth in every religion, even though many people fail to practice it."

"I thought you were a Buddhist, Ray. Are you now going to tell me you're a Christian?"

"No," Ray replied. "I never said I was a Buddhist either."

"You never said it, but I've seen you reading all those books on Buddhism."

"The truth is where you find it," he replied. "I find the same truth in Christianity as I do in Buddhism. I find it in Taoism and Hinduism as well."

"What do you mean?" I asked.

"I think that all religions speak to the same truth. The only difference is in how that truth is conveyed. They use the language and the experience of the people from whom they originated."

I thought about that for a moment. "I don't see how that can be," I said. "Christians say that the only way to heaven is through acceptance of Jesus as your personal savior. I don't think the Buddhists say that."

"No, they don't," Ray answered. "But I don't think Jesus said that either."

"Uh...Ray," I replied, "Jesus said he was the son of God. He also said that 'No one gets to the Father but through me.'"

"Would you like to hear what I think about that?" he asked.

"Sure," I lied. And I began thinking here he goes. Ray is about to get preachy with me. "Are you going to try to save my soul now Ray?" I asked sarcastically.

Ray smiled. His smile was warm, compassionate and friendly. It really pissed me off.

"I am not going to try to save you, Charles," he said. "You don't need anyone to save you."

"Okay," I replied, "Tell me what you think then Ray."

"Forget it," he replied. "You're in one of your moods."

"Will you just fucking tell me what it is you want to say?" I snapped.

Ray stared hard at me. "Are you gonna get off your fucking shit and listen?" he asked, meeting my aggression with his own.

I sighed heavily. "Yeah, Ray," I replied. "I apologize. I'll listen." Cellies often act more like married couples than they would ever be inclined to admit.

"I think it's important that you first understand the history behind the story of Jesus," he said.

"I know the story, Ray."

"I see," Ray replied. "Forget it then, it's not important." Ray picked up his book, laid back on his bunk and began to read. He didn't appear to be angry or irritated, just disinterested.

"No Ray, tell me," I said.

"It's okay Charles. If you already know, you already know. I have no need to say anything."

I was beginning to feel like an ass. "I want to hear what you have to say," I said.

"That's what you said before, then you came back at me with attitude."

"I know, I'm sorry. I'll stop. Please, go on."

Ray laid his book down next to him. "I want you to understand something, Charles," he said.

"What?"

"I want you to know that I am not trying to convince you of anything. I am just trying to tell you some things that helped me make sense of all this. You are free to reject all of it should you choose to do so. I am not going to preach to you."

My experience has been that when someone tells me they are not going to preach to me, what they really mean is they are about to preach to me. But this was Ray, after all, and I had never known him to be preachy. Also I had been an ass twice; I didn't think I could get away with a third attempt. I decided to shut my mouth and give him the benefit of the doubt. But I must say I was guarded. "Go ahead, Ray. I want to hear what you have to say."

Ray sat up on his bunk. "Okay," he said. "Have you ever heard of the ancient Egyptian God named Horus?" He asked.

I furrowed my brow. "What does that have to do with Christians?" I asked.

Ray widened his eyes, tilted his head and stared at me, indicating that I was precariously close to my third attempt.

"Okay," I said. "I'm sorry. No, Ray, I've not heard of Horus."

"Horus was the solar messiah of ancient Egypt," he said. "The earliest records we have of him date from around 3000 BC. It is the story of a child who was born of a virgin on December 25th. He was said to be the son of God. He was a teacher at age twelve. At age thirty, he was baptized and thus began his ministry. He travelled around with twelve disciples performing miracles such as turning water to wine. He was betrayed by one of his disciples, crucified, and after three days, he rose from the dead."

I leaned back and cocked my head. "Really?" I said. "That's the story of Jesus."

"Yes it is," Ray replied. "Only this story was told three thousand years before Jesus was even born."

"You're kidding!"

"No, I'm not. There are many such solar messiahs who share these basic characteristics, told by many different ancient societies. Jesus is only the most recent."

I was stunned. I didn't know what to say.

"It is a story about the sun. It is the sun itself that the Egyptians believed to be the 'Son of God.' It is the sun, or 'son,' that brings the light of God into the world."

"I don't understand," I said. "Do the Christians know this?"

"Most don't," Ray said. "Horus was known as God's only begotten son, the savior of mankind. He was the light and the way. No one came to the Father but through him."

"How can that be?" I asked.

"Because the story is a metaphor. It is a story that tells of an astrological event. The ancients tracked the sun through the sky. They noticed that as winter approached, the days grew shorter, and to them, this symbolized death. They also noticed that the sun moved south as winter progressed. Each morning the sun would rise at a point slightly further south than the day before. This continued until December 22nd, when the sun did a curious thing. It stopped moving south for three days. It did this in the vicinity of a constellation known as the Southern Cross. On December 24th, the three stars in Orion's belt, called the three kings, align with the brightest star in the eastern sky, Sirius, and they pointed to the place where the sun rose on December 25th. On December 25th, the sun moved one degree north, signaling the birth of the new sun. This is why the story says the savior, the sun, died on a cross, was buried for three days, only to rise again. This is also the reality behind the story of the three kings following the star in the east to the birthplace of the sun. This 'birth of the sun' signals the end of winter and the coming of longer days which results in life renewing itself on the planet. It is the story of the cycle of life itself."

"But then, the story of Jesus…"

"The story of Jesus is just a newer version of the very ancient story of Horus, which is itself nothing but a story to illustrate the cycle of the sun, and with it, the cycle of life."

I was stunned. I had never heard this before.

"Now," Ray continued, "keep this story in mind while I tell you what I think about Jesus."

"Okay," I said rather weakly.

"There are those who say that Jesus never really existed; that he is nothing but pure myth. I don't believe that is true. I think he did exist, and I think he had something very important to say…" Ray paused to think. "You know," he continued, "before I go into this, I first have to explain something else to you."

"I'm listening."

Ray considered his words. I could see that he was struggling to find words that would adequately explain the thoughts he was trying to convey. "People today have a very common misperception of what it is to be a human being," he said. "Let me ask you this, Charles. What do you mean when you say that you are a human being?"

I thought about that for a moment. I had never been asked that question before, and I found it difficult to answer. "I'm a man, Ray. I don't know what you mean by that question."

"Precisely," he replied. "This is one of those things that we have been conditioned to believe without really thinking about what it means. What is a human being? When we really think about that question, we seem to be saying that a human being is a skin encapsulated center of conscious awareness."

"Uh…okay…"

"Think about it for a moment Charles," he continued. "You think of this thing you call you, as being everything contained within the boundary of your skin. Everything inside your skin is you; everything outside your skin is other than you."

"Well that seems obvious, Ray."

"It seems obvious because that is what you have been taught. What if what you have been taught is in error?"

"That seems a rather silly question, Ray. I mean, everything inside my skin is me; everything inside of your skin is you."

Ray was struggling to communicate something to me, and I could see his frustration. "Let me try to say it this way," he said. "I want you to assume for a moment that you are not really here at all. You are not even in prison. You are instead at home, asleep in your bed, and you are dreaming all of this. If that were the case, how would you know that you are dreaming?"

"I suppose I wouldn't know," I answered.

"Exactly! You would think all of this is real. And when I said to you that you believe yourself to be that which is enclosed inside of your skin, that would seem real to you as well. But if you are really at home, in bed, asleep and dreaming all of this, then in reality everything is just you. That skin that you think is so real is nothing but a mental projection. Even I would be you, and everything I am saying would be nothing more than you telling yourself all of the things you *think* I am saying. So the idea that you are a skin encapsulated center of consciousness would not be true. You would, in your dream, perceive yourself as such, but in actual fact, there would be no real boundary. Everything would just be you."

"But I'm not dreaming Ray. This is the real world here."

"It seems that way, I know," he said. "But this brings us to what is known as the mystical experience. All of the mystics of every religion have come to an awareness of exactly the same thing. It is described as an experience of awakening, as if from a dream, in which the person comes to know himself as something other than what he had always believed himself to be. Even modern physics has found something very similar here. Matter has no reality at all; it is nothing but an energy vibration. Your body, this thing you think of as you, is in fact nothing more than a consciousness projection manifesting in an energy matrix. That sounds very much like a dream."

Part of me wanted to think that Ray had completely lost it, yet, something about his words resonated deeply in my soul. I wanted to say something profound, deep and meaningful in response, but the words that issued from my mouth were, "So if this is all just a dream, why can't I dream myself out of prison?" So much for my attempt at profound wisdom.

Ray afforded my statement the respect of completely ignoring it. "This is the realization that all the mystics share in common," he continued. "They each express this experience within the confines of the particular religion in which they were raised; therefore, the story is slightly different in each case. But the experience they describe is exactly the same. They awaken to the reality that what they thought of as themselves was just a dream, or an illusion. What they really are is the thing dreaming. And this thing is something infinite and vast, something a finite mind cannot grasp. We call it God for lack of a better term, but even this is limiting. It is as if this thing we call God is one infinite thing expressing itself as each of us. Whereas you dream in terms of only you, this thing called God is capable of dreaming as all people at all times."

"So are you saying we are all God?"

"In a sense, yes. And I think that was what Jesus was saying as well. Think of it this way. Waves on the ocean might very well be tempted to think of themselves as individual waves, separate and distinct from every other wave. Yet in actuality, waves are all manifestations of one ocean."

"So you are saying waves can think?"

An exasperated look came over Ray. "You are just a real asshole sometimes, aren't you?" he asked.

I smiled. "Sorry Ray, it just comes over me. I wouldn't say I am an asshole though. I would say that I am the *whole ass*."

Ray smiled and shook his head.

"Don't sell me short, Ray," I said jokingly.

"This is the realization I think Jesus had," he continued. "He saw himself as a wave, then one day realized he was really ocean. In so doing he also realized that everyone else was ocean too. He was a product of the Judaism of his time, so he spoke in that language when he said, 'I and the Father are one.' It is like the wave saying I and the ocean are one. The people who heard him say this decided to stone him for blasphemy. I mean, here he was claiming to be God. Jesus asked them why they wanted to stone him when he was only saying the very same thing their own God had said. He was referring to the 82nd Psalm, where God says to the people, 'You are gods, you are all sons of the most high.' In that verse, we have God himself saying the very same thing. In the King James Version of the Bible, Jesus goes on to say 'I am the son of god,' and the word 'the' is italicized. Most people mistakenly believe this is for emphasis, as in, 'I am THE son of god,' like Jesus was saying he was the one and only. But italicized words in the Bible actually meant that the word italicized was an interpretation of the original. If you read that verse in the original Greek, you will find Jesus saying, 'I am a son of God.' *A* son, not *the* son. So Jesus was a man just like all the rest of us, who became aware that as men, we are all manifestations of God, just like a wave realizing that all waves are but manifestations of ocean."

"But Christians still say that Jesus is the one and only son of God," I protested.

"Of course they do," Ray replied. "The church that formed around the life of Jesus didn't form until three hundred years later. By then people had built all kinds of legends around the life of this man. And people are lazy. They want Jesus to do it for them. It is as if they think that if they act good enough, they can get into heaven through Jesus. They cling tenaciously to their identity as a wave, never realizing that they are already ocean. People cling to the idea that they are human, never realizing they are already God. Then they write a Bible verse like, 'For ocean so loved the world that it gave its only begotten wave, that whosoever believeth in him shall not perish, but have everlasting life.' They don't want to learn what Jesus actually taught. They want instead to believe that they will live forever as this particular wave. When Jesus said death would lose its sting, he didn't mean that he would go on forever as this particular manifestation known as Jesus. He instead meant that this manifestation of Jesus was an illusion that would return to the God essence that it really was just like an individual wave subsides into the ocean that it really is. When you truly let go of your identity as a wave and you see yourself as the ocean you really are, death becomes an illusion."

"And this is the same thing the Buddhists teach?"

"Essentially, yes, this is what Buddha taught. But like the Christians, the followers of Buddha also wanted to live forever so they began to alter his teaching and came up with the idea of reincarnation, as if this particular manifestation of the self will return again and again. That is nothing but another attempt to live forever as one particular wave. It is ocean that comes back again and again as various waves. It is the God essence that manifests again and again in all things because the God essence is all things."

"So what's the point of it all Ray?'

"There is no point. It is just the God essence doing what it does. It is God Godding, if you will. It is the ocean waving. That's what oceans do. There is no purpose, only meaning. It is the dance, as the Hindus say, it is the dance of Shiva. The idea is to surrender to it, not to try to make sense of it. In that you will find peace."

"Wow!" I said. It was all I could think to say.

"So give the Christians a break," Ray said. "They have the right idea. They just have to learn to apply it correctly. All any religion can do is point to the truth. It is up to the individual to embrace that truth. To do so, one finds that one must go beyond the precepts that the religion will allow. The Bible will only carry you as far as it can. From there you must make the ultimate leap of faith, transcend even the Bible, and trust the spirit of God within you; trust that which you already are. Bible worship is a very dangerous form of idolatry. The ultimate act of faith, the ultimate act of following the will of God, is considered by men to be an act of heresy. They killed Jesus for doing it."

"So the story of Jesus?"

"Men took the memory of Jesus, then they put his name in place of Horus. That was a political decision, nothing more. Constantine needed to reunify a divided Rome and determined this was the best way to do it. Thus, he created the Catholic Church."

"Are you saying the church is bad?"

"No, not at all. It is a tool to aid in this realization just as the Bible is. The truth is there for those who can see it. The truth is everywhere. When you see it, you will see through good and evil, straight into that which simply is. All else simply is not."

Ray abruptly turned off the light and stopped talking. I had so many questions racing through my mind, but he left me alone with them. This was typical of Ray. He said what he had to say, and he could care less what I thought of it. It was as if he knew that the rest was up to me. I actually liked that about him, even though it irritated me. He allowed me the freedom to think whatever I wanted. He seemed to feel no need to convince me of anything. He knew that the words he spoke did not need him to defend them. It was a very long time before I could fall asleep.

CHAPTER NINE

If thou wilt make a man happy, add not unto his riches but take away from his desires. – Epicurus

Prison went from bad to worse. I was walking in the day hall headed back to my cell one day when I rounded a corner that took me out of view from the guard tower. I had walked this path many times before so it now became a habit that I gave little thought. As I rounded the corner, BLAM! A fist smashed into my right eye. Before I had any concept of what was happening, two men were beating, kicking and punching me. The first punch stunned me, and from that moment on, fists seem to be coming at me from every direction. There was nothing I could do but stand there and take the beating. I never fell, never went to the ground. It was violent, brutal. My body went numb. Time slowed until it became non-existent. I took blow after blow, and it felt as if it was happening to someone else. It seemed to last forever, and it seemed to last only a moment. In fact, it was over very quickly. Prison attacks are like that: fast and horribly violent. The attackers have to inflict maximum damage in the shortest possible time, then run away so they will not get caught.

I staggered into the day hall bleeding profusely, vaguely aware of my surroundings. I stumbled about as everyone watched me. I remember little from then on. The alarm sounded and uniformed guards swarmed about me slamming me to the ground, cuffing my hands behind my back. It didn't matter that I was the victim of the attack. I was treated as if I was the attacker. When my mind finally cleared, I was in the infirmary. Three broken ribs, a broken orbital socket around my right eye, a bruised liver and a concussion rounded out my injury list. The beating was bad, but it was nothing compared to the hell I was about to experience.

The following day I was taken from the infirmary to an interview room. I was told to sit in a chair as three uniformed guards surrounded me. Prison changes people; it makes them hard and calloused. The guards are not exempt. They are in prison too, and the environment changes them. In many subtle ways, they view the inmates as less than human. The violence they inflict is not overt—they never beat me or physically harmed me in any way. No, the violence they inflicted was far more subtle and far more insidious than that. They deprived me of the basic respect one would afford any human being, forever reminding me that, to them, I was no longer human. Most people would afford a dog far more compassion than these people afforded me.

You learn to look at a guard's collar to determine his rank. The man who brought me into the room and sat me in the chair now stood guard by the door. His collar had nothing on it, signifying his rank as a corrections officer or C.O. The man to my left had the silver pin attached to his collar signifying Sergeant. The man to my right had the silver Lieutenant bar on his collar. And the man seated in the chair in front of me had the double bar telling me he was a Captain. He was running this show. The scene felt staged; as if they had done this hundreds of times before.

"Beat you pretty badly?" the Captain asked with a fake air of concern.

"Yes sir," I replied.

"You know, they are likely to come back and finish the job when I release you to general population tomorrow," he continued. I stared at him saying nothing. "I want to help you," he said. "I need you to tell me who did this to you."

It's difficult to adequately describe what I was going through at that moment. Many conflicting urges pulled at me from every direction. I feared I would be killed as soon as I was returned to my unit. I was concerned that to survive, I may have to kill or otherwise harm one or both of the men who did this to me. I had already met people who had come to prison with relatively short sentences who, in order to survive, had to do things that resulted in new charges and extra years that now had to be served. I lived in constant fear of that. There was something else going on in me that was far more subtle, and far more dangerous. We are conditioned throughout our lives to want to turn to those in authority for help when we are seriously harmed. This conditioning, reinforced by fear, compelled me to look to these men for help, to believe they could protect me, to believe that they really did care about me. I wanted so badly to tell them what had happened, to believe that they wanted to protect me from further harm. My entire being longed to believe that they saw me as a human being in need of help and that they valued me enough to do something to make all of this better. I almost spoke. I almost told the Captain what he wanted to know. Almost, until my survival instinct stepped in. "Tell them, and you're dead," it told me. I stared at the Captain, saying nothing.

He sighed deeply as he leaned back in his chair. The Sergeant then chimed in. "Just throw him back in with the wolves and let them have him, Captain," he said. "This piece of shit wants to protect the people who are going to kill him, so let them kill him. He doesn't deserve to live anyway."

My heart beat forcefully. Panic surged through my veins. I struggled to fight it down, to cope. My purely animal instinct was on full alert and I wanted to run, to escape, to somehow change the reality that now confronted me. But this reality would not change. No one would protect me. There was nowhere to run, nowhere to hide. Desperation became absolute. I wanted to wake up. I wanted this to all be a dream. But it was not a dream. The world spun about me in a dance of pure madness. My mind trembled like a string stretched to the point of snapping. I could taste the fear on the sides of my tongue and at the back of my mouth. Sweat poured from my forehead. Thoughts raced through my mind; scream, cry, shout, run, hide, escape, anything to revolt against a reality I could not do a damned thing about. "This can't be real," I thought. But it was real. My God, how did I ever wind up here?

"Breathe Charles, just breathe," I told myself. "Tell them nothing. They won't help you. They don't care about you. They will arrest the two who did this, throw you back in gen pop, where you will be killed for snitching. Talk and you're dead…talk and you're dead…" I repeated this to myself over and over. It was the only thing I had to hang on to.

The Captain leaned forward in his chair, his face moving within inches of mine. The fake friendliness he showed me only a moment before transformed into what he truly felt about me. It was the look he might give to the dog shit he just stepped in and was now wiping off the bottom of his shoe. "You listen to me, you sorry fuck," he said. "You're going to tell me what I want to know or I will throw you in the hole. You will stay there until you tell me."

I hated him now. Thank God for that hatred and that anger. It was both a comforting blanket and a protective suit of armor. Seething hatred. It was mine. It was something they could not take away from me. It was the only expression of me that was allowed, and I at last had found it. It would save me. It would protect me.

Hatred welled up from the depths of my soul and shot like fire from my eyes. "Fuck you, you low-life piece of shit," I replied with the voice of the Devil himself. I no longer wanted to run. I no longer wanted to alter my reality. I wanted one thing and one thing only. I wanted to kill. I wanted to kill everything and everyone. My body trembled with rage. I was anger incarnate. Hatred was my immortal God.

"Throw him in the hole," the Captain said. "You can stay there till you rot."

I had finally given voice to the demon burning inside me. I let out a scream of anger so violent, so animal, so purely carnal that the hairs over my entire body stood fully erect. I was no longer human. I had become something primal. The power of unadulterated hatred surged through my being. Nothing would ever harm me again. I would kill, without thought, anything that tried. I was now hatred incarnate and I reveled in the power of it as the guards dragged me to the hole.

• • •

Human beings are, by nature, very social animals. We were not meant to live in isolation. I had heard this often; now I was about to live it. Twenty-three hour a day lockdown, completely alone. No one to talk to. No television, no radio. There is nothing like it. It would be impossible for me to explain it. You would have to live it to fully understand. It was there that I learned how badly we humans seek to escape from ourselves through distraction. To be confronted with nothing but yourself is pure terror.

The only break in the monotony was one hour yard time each day, and three times a week I could leave my cell to shower. "Yard time" is a euphemism. What it really meant was one hour to go outside and be locked in a six foot by ten foot chain link enclosure that is basically a dog kennel. The cage was mounted on concrete, and was about eight feet high with a chain link ceiling. There was nothing to do but pace around in a circle for an hour then go back to my cell. I did that once, then decided I would not allow them to treat me like a dog so as to afford themselves the illusion that they were in any way treating me humanely.

My only time out of the cell was to shower three times a week. This was an adventure. Hands behind my back placed through the slot in the door so I could be cuffed. Door opens and two guards escort me to the showers. All movement required a two guard escort. The shower resembled a stainless steel coffin stood on end. I was locked in. I then placed my hands through a slot in the door and my cuffs were removed. I showered in an enclosure so narrow I could barely lift my arms. When I was through, I shouted to the guards. I could find myself standing there twenty minutes or longer before they came. Hands through the slot, cuffs on wrists, door opens, escort back to cell, hands through slot, cuffs removed. That was the extent of my human contact. Soon I began attempting to engage them in conversation. They didn't hear me. They were immune to my humanity. I was nothing but an animate piece of flesh to be transported. No one heard me. No one saw me. I didn't really exist.

The auditory hallucinations kicked in at about two weeks. I began hearing music that was not there. At first I thought one of the guards was playing a radio, but then I noticed that the volume of the music was the same even when I covered my ears. This was maddening after a time. I couldn't shut out the sound. The lighting never changed. Day was as night, and night was as day. No clock or watch to help keep track of time. Only the feeding schedule distinguished morning, noon and night. Never enough food. Constant hunger. Cell kept uncomfortably cold. No blanket to keep warm. It was, in a word, torture. Not the torture of the infliction of physical pain. It was instead the subtle torture of relentless discomfort. I cannot imagine what form of human mind invented such a thing.

Time lost all meaning. I paced and exercised in my cell in an attempt to break the monotony. Hundreds upon hundreds of pushups, sit-ups and the like, in the hope that exhaustion would bring sleep. One of the most insidious effects of the time spent in the hole was the complete disconnect from anything resembling the cycles of nature. It was a completely artificial world; an artificial existence. I was alone, in a timeless reality of living death. However, I did have paper and a pencil. On the thirtieth day, I wrote this poem.

> *They drain everything of its texture, its color.*
> *White, gray, concrete, steel.*
> *The essence of everything living is gone.*
> *Social isolation, physical isolation.*
> *One small window my only contact with the organic, living world,*
> *And through that I can see but a small patch of blue, a twig of green,*
> *And more concrete and steel.*
> *For thirty days I sit alone in my concrete enclosure.*
> *No human contact save the passing of a meal tray three times a day.*
> *One hour out of my cell to shower, to do nothing else*
> *But step into a slightly larger concrete and steel enclosure.*
> *Still no one to talk to, nothing to see.*
> *I am the only life I see in my concrete hell.*
> *I read, sleep eat. My mind wanders a bit more each day.*
> *I hear the tortured screams and anguished cries of others as they shout and wail*
> *Moan and cry angry taunts to no one, to nothing.*
> *I wonder how long they have endured this.*
> *How long before I become as they,*
> *Shouting angry obscenities to a world that cannot hear.*

*Professing angrily that I am still alive, still here despite all
    evidence to the contrary.*
For what proof have I that I am still living?
What living thing assures me that I still am?
How long before I too scream that I am a living thing?
Scream to no one who can hear...
*Will I assert my existence in a futile effort to convince concrete
    and steel*
That I am real...that I matter?
The concrete and steel do not care.
They will only respond with cold, hard indifference.
Only thirty days have I endured this hell.
How many more till my mind snaps?
Am I really here? Yes!
How do I know?
*Because the agony of isolation reminds me that I must still be
    alive.*
The torment of white and gray, concrete and steel, cold and hard,
Loneliness and utter isolation scream at me telling me I am alive.
Alive in the sense that my heart beats, my blood flows.
Alive but not living.
White and gray
One endlessly eternal day.
Agony without joy.
Life without color, texture, softness, warmth.
Living death.

This had become my life, my existence. My mind slowly slipping away. I was aware that my mind was leaving me, but I was powerless to do anything to stop it. The music in my head eventually subsided into a constant background melody that began to comfort me in my isolation. I often found it difficult to discern between my sleeping dreams and my time awake. I was dissolving. Before long, I simply sat and stared, numb, dead.

Then, on the forty-fifth day, my cell door opened. "Time to go," the guard said with no further explanation. I said nothing. I stood and walked out, no cuffs, a single guard to escort me. I was taken back to my cell with Ray. It was nighttime, lockdown. I shuffled into my cell, climbed onto my bunk and cried.

That night Ray did a funny thing. He got out of his bunk, walked over to mine, sat beside me and placed his hand on my shoulder. "It's okay, my brother," he said. "You made it. You survived. The bastards want to break you. Hell, they want to destroy everything about you, but you made it." I rolled over and hugged him. I so badly longed for human contact that I no longer cared that this was a man, a convict. He was flesh and blood and I needed human touch, any human touch. And Ray, to his credit, held me, comforted me. "It's okay, my friend," he reassured me. "It's all over now. Things will be better tomorrow." He held me for some time then returned to his bunk and went to sleep. I laid awake for many hours, my head spinning. Exhaustion at last came over me, and I drifted off to sleep.

The man who walked out of the hole that evening was not the same man who walked in. Every last ounce of anything living in me had died. My only remaining thought was that there was unfinished business to be handled, and I was going to handle it. When the buzzer sounded for breakfast, I walked straight to the cell of one of the men who had attacked me. I didn't care about the consequences. I didn't care if the guards saw me. I now fully understood the insanity of prison. I had to handle this, or else I would be a marked man and everyone would target me. I caught him by surprise as he was leaving his cell and hit him square in the nose before he knew what had happened. As he fell back, I pounced upon him, swinging my fists like a mad man. My pent up anger and hatred spewed forth upon him as I unleashed a violent fury like nothing I ever imagined could have come out of me.

And yet I wasn't feeling anything. It was as if I had become two people. One, a vicious and wild animal violently attacking another human being. The other, a passive observer who could not feel anything, and therefore did not care about what was happening. I kept beating the man long after he was unable to defend himself. I would have killed him had it not been for Ray. Ray seemed to know what was up, and he followed me as I went to the inmate's cell. He pulled me off the man and instructed me to get on to the chow hall. To this day, I don't know why I didn't get caught. I suppose in the commotion of everyone filing out for chow, the guards simply did not see me. In any event, I had made my statement: Fuck with me and there would be hell to pay.

I ran into the other guy who attacked me when I arrived at the chow hall. He was already aware of what had happened to his partner. I decided I liked the table where he was seated, so I took a seat directly across from him. I sat down, saying nothing. I stared directly into his eyes. My eyes exuded a dead hatred, dispassionate, filled with pure evil. I immediately saw the fear in his eyes. This excited me, and my excitement manifested as a slight grin on my face. I can only imagine what I must have looked like. The color that drained from his face told me that I must have appeared as an absolute mad man. I decided to speak.

"I am going to kill you," I said. The sound of my voice surprised even me. Never had such a sound come out of me before. It was icy cold. And it carried an absolute sense of confidence. I spoke the words so calmly that the man sitting before me had no doubt I would make good on my word. Fortunately for me, and even more so for him, he pulled what was called a check-in move. He refused to leave the chow hall and return to his unit. This meant he would be taken to the hole. It is what people sometimes do in prison, yet to do so labels you a coward. I don't know what happened to him after that. Apparently he was transferred somewhere else because I never saw him again.

From that day on, my prison experience changed. I had developed a reputation for being someone who would hit back and hit back hard if you fucked with me. This carried a great deal of respect. I also had won the added respect of the inmates by doing my hole time and not snitching to the guards. I was no longer a fish. I was now a shark, and everyone knew how dangerous a shark I had become.

Ray was on his bunk when I returned to my cell. Life was very different for me now. I could sense things I was never able to sense before. It was as if I could feel the energy emanating from a person, and that energy spoke to me. I could feel Ray's energy. He was nervous now. He knew that I was angry and unstable. It can be very dangerous to be locked in a cell with someone like me. I also knew Ray wanted to say something but did not know if he should do so. I stared at him for a few moments, then I spoke.

"You have something to say to me?" I asked, and again I was surprised by the sound of my own voice. I sounded mean, hard.

Ray stared back at me as he considered his words. "You're letting them beat you," he said.

"How's that?" I asked.

"You've become an animal," he replied. "I've seen this before. Animals don't fare so well in here. They get caught up with new charges. You're lucky no one saw you today."

"I did what I had to do," I answered.

"I understand you did what you had to do, but you were careless." Ray was clearly worried. But his worry seemed more for me than for him. I became angry with him and wanted to tell him to mind his own fucking business. But he pulled me off that man earlier and probably saved me from a murder charge. I felt I owed him, so I would give him a pass. "Charles," Ray continued, "The question you have to ask yourself is this: is the man you are now the man you want to be?"

"I am the man I have to be," I replied sharply.

"No, that's not true," Ray responded. "You did what you had to do. But this is not what you have to be."

"I don't understand." Ray's words made no sense to me. "I have to be what I've become in order to do what I did."

"Do you?" Ray asked. He leaned forward on his bunk and stared deeply into me. "You are now confronted with the reality of prison," he said. "That reality meant that you had to beat up the guys who attacked you, or else you would have been everyone's little bitch in here. That's just the way things are, and that's the shit you have to deal with. You did that and did that well, even though you were careless. You dealt with the reality that confronted you, but you don't have to *become* that reality. There is a subtle distinction to be made here. Can you engage the world without losing yourself in that world?"

Ray's words still made no sense to me, and yet, deep inside, they somehow seemed familiar. It was as if his words carried a truth I could feel even though I could not understand. He saw my confusion.

"It's like this Charles," he continued. "Sometimes the world forces our hand, and we have to act accordingly. We don't always have a choice about that. What we can choose is whether or not we are going to let those actions define who we are. Are you going to be the violent animal you became today? Or are you going to be you, Charles, the man you've always been, choosing to engage violence from time to time because you have to in order to survive? On the one hand, you can remain true to yourself while doing whatever it is life requires of you. On the other hand, you get sucked in, and you lose yourself. If that happens, you will become whatever it is you feel you have to do, and what you will become Charles, is a monster."

Something about his words hit me hard. I knew, deep inside, that I didn't want to be what I had become, but I felt it was necessary in order to survive. And the respect I had won from the other inmates created in me a newfound desire to become the monster Ray spoke of. This last thought prompted my response. "But everyone out there respects me now. They are already treating me differently. I like the fact that they are afraid of me now."

"That's how your environment reinforces the total loss of your self," he answered. "You can walk around out there feeling big and bad. You *were* walking around scared of your own shadow; now you can walk around feeling invincible. That's your ego talking. It's convincing you that being a monster is a good thing. You're letting your environment shape who you are, as opposed to choosing what you want to be. I'm telling you Charles, this environment will turn you into something horrible if you let it. Like it or not, you are tempted into doing this because of fear. You think this inflation of your ego is the solution to your fear. I assure you, it's not."

"I'm not afraid of anything," I stated flatly.

"Keep telling yourself that Charles. No matter how many times you repeat it, you'll never actually believe it." He paused for a moment to think, and then said, "You know Charles, people who react to fear are defined by it. Courage is not a reaction to fear, it is a response."

I stared hard at Ray as he picked up his book, laid back on his bunk, and began to read. I did not know it at the time but a seed had been planted in my mind. It was a seed that would one day sprout and grow, bearing the sweetest fruit imaginable. I still had no idea what it was Ray was trying to tell me. But whatever it was, it had caused a deep disturbance in my soul. It contained a truth I was utterly blind to. But it was there just the same. One day I would come to know what that truth was.

Charles Bynum

CHAPTER TEN

All intelligent thoughts have already been thought; what is necessary is only to try to think them again. – Johann Wolfgang von Goethe

Things were very different for me over the next few months. Prison was becoming more tolerable. I had almost come to enjoy the fear I instilled in others, or more accurately, I had come to enjoy the sense of power. I had proven myself in a difficult situation. I remembered watching movies where the lead character was in prison, and I had wondered how I would handle things if I found myself in such a situation. Now I knew the answer to that question, and I was proud of my performance.

It is rather absurd as I look back on it now. I was enjoying a new found sense of power, yet I was living in an environment where I was stripped of all power. I am often amazed at the tricks my mind will play in order to delude itself. I had no power of any kind, yet I created the illusion of power through the manipulation of fear—mine and others. I had learned a foolish little equation. Ego applied to fear equals power. That is, of course, my ego applied to the fear of another. It was an exploitative form of expression. From there I came to the conclusion that power was thus the cure for fear. Let me be clear here. This was my ego applied to the fear of another as a cure for my fear. To lessen my own fear, I had to exacerbate the fear of another human being. This led me into the temptation of intimidation. It worked like this: I was feeling afraid. In order to deny the fear exists, I sought someone weaker than me. I then set out to intimidate or harm that person in the hope that he would fear me. His fear of me gave me a sense of power over him. That sense of power reinforced my ego, thereby temporarily numbing my fear. There you have it. That is prison in a nutshell. Fear drives everything, and egos inflict all manner of harm upon one another in response.

Sounds like an insane world, doesn't it? It is insane, but not all that unique. People like to keep things filed away in neat little categories. There is prison, and there is the real world. These are two separate and distinct environments, right? Wrong. Prison is nothing but an extreme example of what is happening everywhere in the world. People are people. The environment cannot bring out of people anything that is not already in them. An extreme environment will bring out existing tendencies in an extreme way. But look around. Isn't everyone in the world more or less driven by fear? Aren't people caught in myriad little power struggles with one another? Isn't everyone searching for a sense of safety and a sense of peace in an otherwise threatening and hostile environment? Your world may not be prison. But it is not likely freedom either.

Prison helped me see the world, and myself, differently. And by differently, I mean more accurately, with greater clarity. In prison I no longer had any need of rationalizations. This was a very important point. In prison I asserted my power over others because that is what I wanted to do. I made no excuses and no effort to hide it. In the real world, we tend to do these things covertly. Engaging this behavior in prison opened my eyes to the fact that I had done the exact same thing in the real world, albeit more subtly. In that world, too, I attempted to assert my power over others. Let me give you an example. Let's say in a relationship with a woman, I one day began to feel insecure. Now let's assume that what triggered this insecurity was that she smiled at another man in a way that was, to me, just a bit too friendly. A conflict then develops in my mind. The childish, insecure, fear-driven part of my mind immediately shouts, "She wants to fuck him." The more mature part of my mind says, "Don't be ridiculous. She is just a friendly person who smiles warmly at everyone. That's one of the things you love about her." There is a war now being waged in my mind, though I likely do not see it as such. I will deny my childish thought without fully acknowledging it, because I do not want to think of myself as someone who could think so foolishly. That childish person is not who I want to be, so I just ignore it, deny it. But here's the rub. That childish person *is* a part of me, whether I like it or not. That part of me demands acknowledgement. If it does not get it, it will find its way out one way or another.

So here I am caught in this insecure state of mind. What is insecurity? It is one particular manifestation of fear. So I am feeling fear, yet I do not want to acknowledge that fear. And as is always the case, unacknowledged fear will seek expression by driving my behavior. Before I know it, I am angry or irritated with her for some small little nothing that makes no sense. My unacknowledged fear seeks expression, but I am not aware of this. I've denied the fear so I do not believe it can be driving my behavior. Now she and I are driving home, I am seething with anger but I don't know why. I am waiting for her to do something, anything so I can vent this anger. And she inevitably commits, what is to me, some horrible transgression. She will do something like roll the car window down while I have the air conditioning on and that will be all it takes. "How many times have I told you to keep the windows up while the AC is running..." She looks at me like I'm a fool, having no idea why I'm making such an issue out of nothing. I have no idea why I'm making such an issue out of nothing. I may even realize in the back of my mind that I am being ridiculous, but at this moment, I am powerless to stop it.

Now here's the contradiction. This began because I had a childish, immature thought that I believed to be beneath me. I refused to acknowledge that thought, but it didn't go away, leaving me to behave in a most childish way. That childish fear found expression. I found the excuse I needed to attack and punish the woman who I believe caused that fear to manifest in me. But I am acting completely outside of awareness. My conscious mind has no idea what is going on. It is as if some automatic program has taken over my body, and I am being pulled blindly along. My attempt to avoid childish behavior brought about the very behavior I sought to avoid.

In prison I was freed from all such rationalizations. I acted as I was moved to act because that is how I wanted to act. No need to hide or justify anything. This fact is the only difference. In the real world, my fear drove me to act, but the image of myself that I wanted to maintain forced that action to be driven outside of my awareness. In prison, I simply acted as I wanted to act, remaining ever aware of what I was doing. What I did not yet realize in either case was the extent to which fear drove all of my behaviors. What I was beginning to see was how rationalizations and denial allowed me to engage in behaviors without having to assume responsibility for those behaviors. Living in an environment where such rationalizations were no longer necessary allowed me to see how I used such rationalizations in the real world.

Rationalizations are a dirty business. They are the means by which we maintain an image of ourselves that contradicts what we really are. The most selfish acts are reconstructed in the mind so that they appear to be altruistic acts of kindness. Or, as is often the case, cruelty is reconstructed into justice. Either way, rationalizations are a barrier to personal growth. Abandoning them allowed me to act as I wanted, but it forced me to look at what I had become. I became engaged in a kind of honest cruelty. And I no longer made any attempt to see it as anything other than what it was.

I began paying closer attention to Ray. Something about Ray was unlike the other inmates. He walked about with a calm sense of detachment. He seemed friendly to everyone, close to no one. He spoke to me about things which, even though they didn't make sense to me, still somehow seemed compelling. Ray was one of the most intelligent and educated men I have ever known. I couldn't figure out why he was in prison. How could a man like Ray have done anything so horrible that he would have to spend the remainder of his life in prison? This made no sense. And Ray seemed to have seen something that other people never see. It was this "something" that he was attempting to show me, though so far I was unable to see. So I began to observe him to see if I could determine just what it was he was talking about. I also half suspected that I would learn that he was full of shit—talked a good game and that would be all.

That was not what I learned. The more I paid attention to Ray, the more intrigued I became. He seemed to meet every situation that confronted him exactly as the situation required. If, for example, a person decided to pop off and behave aggressively toward Ray, Ray would meet that aggression with an assertiveness that diffused the situation, as opposed to escalating it. He handled every situation with expert precision. Nothing rattled him. It seemed to me that he was able to do this because he never took anything personally. It was as if he was free to act however he felt was most effective in any situation, because he didn't have his emotions tied into anything.

Ray was constantly observing everything. He even observed me observing him. At first I thought he was slightly paranoid, but there was no fear or paranoia in his observations. He was just watching, paying attention to everything that was going on around him, detached, emotionally un-invested. The more I watched him, the more I became aware that Ray was a man who seemed more at peace than any man I had ever known. He was always calm, no matter what was going on around him. This, more than anything else, intrigued me.

I, on the other hand, was still running around thinking I was a badass. I was emotionally invested in everything, and my life was nothing but pure prison drama. I observed everything around me just as Ray did, but I did so from a place of constant fear. I wanted to know all the angles so I could predict where the next threat might come from. Ray never seemed to worry about where the next threat would come from. He just dealt with whatever came when it came. My life was a constant roller-coaster ride of emotional highs and lows. Ray's life was one of continued peace. And the strange thing was you could feel that peace flowing out of him. People seemed to feel better when Ray was around.

My life was fast spinning out of control. Violence begets violence, and my acts of violence were already setting the tone, creating a future replete with more of that which I was now indulging. Looking back, I am amazed at how blind I was to my participation in creating the reality that was unfolding before me. I thought life just did things, and I had to react. I simply could not see the extent to which life is an interaction. Life flows in whatever direction it flows, while at the same time it interacts with the energy I put out, forming itself in whatever way it must to teach me whatever it is I am to learn. I now thought of myself as a prison badass. Such a life is a life of constant danger, constant fear, constant threat. And that was what my life had become. I thought life had done this to me; I was simply playing the hand I had been dealt. But life had done no such thing. I chose this. Each new moment, I was choosing it again. Every moment offered me the opportunity to choose a different life, and yet I repeatedly chose this one. Life was giving me exactly what I was asking of it. That's what life does. It gives you whatever it is you choose. The trick is to become aware of the fact that you are choosing.

I felt as if some great calamity was looming somewhere in my immediate future, though I had no idea what I could do to stave it off. I lived in a constant state of anxiety and agitation. I was a slave to my emotions. My emotions surged, and I reacted. I found myself forever at the mercy of whatever I happened to be feeling at the moment. And there I was in close proximity to Ray, who by contrast, seemed always at peace no matter what was going on around him. His emotions did not have the power over him that mine had over me. I got irritated with Ray. It was an irritation born of envy. I longed for the peace he seemed to possess. I was beginning to see that my prison badass role was not bringing me the relief that I thought it would. In fact, it was the opposite. My new role was only adding to my sense of fear and apprehension, just as Ray told me it would. I realized more and more each day that Ray saw something I was unable to see. I wanted to see it too.

A gang war broke out in the prison. The Northsiders and the Sorrenos popped off in the yard one day. The Mexican gangs hated each other and were forever getting into such skirmishes. Violence, brutality, beatings, stabbings, blood and gore. Yawn. The alarm sounded and everyone hit the ground. Yawn again. It was just more of the same. Men shackled and taken off to the hole. The rest of us herded into our respective cells for twenty-four hour lockdown. No more yard time. No more wandering out in the day hall. No more chow hall. Meals would be brought to our cells. This time we would be locked down for two weeks. Life had lost its flavor. Even violence failed to interest me anymore.

After about a week, I was getting stir crazy, wanting out of my cell. Ray was his usual calm self. "Don't you want out of here?" I asked, irritated by his serenity.

"I try not to want anything anymore," he replied.

"I don't understand you, Ray."

"What don't you understand, Charles?"

"Have you just been in here so long that you've lost all zest for life?"

"Quite the contrary," Ray replied. "I am at perfect peace with life."

I scowled. "You're in prison, Ray."

"I know where I am."

"How can you say you're at peace while you're in prison?"

Ray paused to consider his words. "Charles, there is really no point in answering your question. You won't hear me no matter what I say."

"Try me," I replied.

"Ok, Charles. Do you think your sense of peace is dependent upon your environment?"

"What do you mean?" I asked.

"I mean, does the world out there have anything to do with whether or not you feel at peace?"

"Well…sure it does," I replied. "It is a violent and dangerous world out there. No one can be at peace in the midst of such a world."

"I am at peace," Ray stated flatly.

"Yeah, but I'm beginning to think you've lost your mind," I said smiling.

Ray smiled. "You don't know how true that statement really is," he said. "I had to lose my mind in order to find me."

I stared at him, a confused look on my face.

"I told you, you wouldn't understand," he said.

"Well, help me then," I protested.

Ray kept smiling. It was a mesmerizing smile of peace, contentment and confidence. If he was crazy, I wanted to be as crazy as him.

"Have you ever seen a cactus, Charles?"

That seemed a strange question. "What the fuck?" I said.

"Just answer me, Charles."

"Have I ever seen a cactus?"

"Yes. Have you ever seen a cactus?"

"Yes, Ray. I have seen a cactus. What that has to do with anything…"

"A cactus is a very violent plant," he interrupted. "It will inflict great harm upon you. But it will only inflict the violence upon you that you inflict upon it. It is a very impersonal form of violence. The cactus means you no harm. It is just being a cactus. The violence that occurs is not an attack of one life form upon another. It is instead an interaction. For the violence to occur, you must interact *with* the cactus."

He said nothing more. I kept waiting for him to finish, to make his point, but no more words came. And, as usual, what he said made no sense at all.

"Ok," I replied. "So touch a cactus and you get stuck. What does that have to do with anything?"

"Exactly, Charles. What does that have to do with *everything*?"

Ray often irritated me like this. He would say stupid shit that made no sense, then follow up with a stupid question that also made no sense. Yet I knew it somehow made sense to him, and because I couldn't understand it, I got upset. Then he would sit there and smile and I would just feel stupid. Fuck him.

"Would you stop speaking in riddles and tell me whatever it is you're trying to say?" I protested.

"Life is like that cactus, Charles," he answered. "It is going to react to whatever you do to it."

Something deep inside me stirred, yet I could not get my mind around what he was saying.

"You'll never get your mind around it, Charles," Ray said.

Great! He was reading my fucking mind now. I cannot adequately describe the depth of my frustration. It was like trying to thread a needle with thread that was too thick for an eye that was too small with fingers that were too fat and a hand that kept shaking. I wanted to get it. I knew I should be able to get it. But I couldn't get it. I sighed.

"Have I ever told you about the South Indian Monkey Trap, Charles?" he asked.

"Here we go," I thought. "No Ray, you never told me about that."

"The villagers in the southern part of India like to eat the monkeys that live there. To catch them, the people have devised this ingenious trap. They take a coconut and hollow it out by drilling a small hole. Then they fill the coconut with a sweetened rice mixture. They attach a three foot long chain to the coconut and attach the other end of the chain to a stake that they drive into the ground. They then leave the trap and wait.

"Apparently the monkeys in that region like to eat the sweet rice. Soon a monkey will come down from the trees and stick its hand in the coconut to get some of the rice. But the hole in the coconut is just big enough for the monkey to get its hand inside. Once it grabs the rice into a fist, it can no longer get its hand out of the coconut. The villagers then come with clubs, intending to beat the monkey to death so they can eat it for dinner.

"Now the monkey sees the villagers coming and is terrified. It screams and yells and attempts to run, but it can't get away. Its hand is caught in the trap. All that monkey has to do is let go of the rice and his hand will pop right out and he will be free. But the monkey wants that rice. He doesn't want to let go. And as the villagers approach, his fear is so great that he forgets that the only thing trapping him is his own desire. His fear makes him look outside of himself for the solution to his problem. He sees the villagers coming and he is terrified. He runs this way, and he runs that way, but he is attached to a three foot tether. The villagers descend upon him and beat him to death. He dies never realizing that he was the ultimate cause of his own death. Then, to add insult to injury, as he dies, his hand relaxes and falls right out of the coconut."

I sat transfixed, not knowing what to say.

"We human beings are as dumb as that monkey," Ray continued. "You, Charles, are as dumb as that monkey. You are looking outside yourself for a solution that can only be found within. The situation around you is fraught with danger; therefore you are seeking resolution from that danger by looking at the situation around you. You will not find the resolution there. You must turn your focus within and discover how your desire for that sweet tasting rice has you caught in this trap. The trap, Charles, requires your explicit participation to keep you trapped. Without you, it can do nothing."

Ray's words that day spoke to something deep inside of me. Those words precipitated a subtle yet profound change in my being. From that day forward, I looked more and more inside of me for the answer to whatever problems life presented. I wasn't very good at it yet, but I was trying. When something caused me stress or irritation, I searched inside myself for whatever I had contributed to the situation. I was looking to see if I had my hand in a coconut. I began to see that in every instance, I did something to contribute to the situation. It was that part, my part, that I could assert some influence over. I was slowly becoming aware of my true power.

I also continued observing Ray. I began to see things in him that I had never noticed before. Everywhere he went, and in everything he did, he exuded a confident sense of inner peace. I also noticed how people reacted to him. Some of the most violent and evil men I had ever known, reacted toward Ray with a softness that one would never think them capable of. It was as if his inner peace infected those around him. I also noticed that people sought him out when they were having difficulties. They talked to him and opened up to him in ways I could not imagine them doing with anyone else. I saw that contact with Ray made a person's life just a little bit better, their suffering a little bit less. Ray had a healing effect on everyone.

Ray did something else that I thought odd. He liked to meditate. He would sit for hours, alone in his cell, and do nothing. This was something I did not understand. I thought it a stupid thing to do, but I had not asked him about it. It was his thing, and I thought it best to leave him to it.

Ray was also very perceptive. He always seemed to know what was on my mind. If I was troubled, he knew it. If I was happy, he knew that also. It was strange, but I almost felt as if I were naked in front of him. I couldn't hide anything. I never met a man so aware of everything that was going on around him. It irritated me sometimes. He would point out to me things that I would rather not look at. But he was never judgmental. He just observed things without attaching labels such as "right" or "wrong," "good" or "bad" to them. To Ray, everything was either helpful or not helpful, that's all. Some things were conducive to inner peace, some were not. And he never seemed concerned with why. He didn't try to figure things out. Things just were what they were, and he dealt with them as they were.

"It seems to me that your eyes are beginning to open, Charles," Ray said to me one evening after lockdown. He did this often. He would suddenly engage me in a conversation for, what appeared to me to be, no particular reason.

"What do you mean?" I asked.

"You don't seem to be as angry as you were before," he said.

I thought about that for a moment. He was right. The shift had been so subtle that I had not been aware of it. But things didn't irritate me as badly, or as often, as they had before.

"You are beginning to disengage," he continued.

"Disengage?" I asked.

"From all of the external chatter around you," he replied. "All of that stuff going on around you is just stuff. The more you begin to see that the real cause of your suffering is not what is going on around you, but is instead what is taking place within you, the less enamored you are with the external world."

Ray was continuing with his strange habit of saying things that didn't quite make sense to me. I sometimes wondered if he did this for sport, as a means of killing time. But it no longer frustrated me. I stopped trying to understand everything he said, and started to listen more. I still asked questions and engaged in conversation, but there was no longer the desperate need to understand. Understanding was no longer something I felt compelled to force. It was something I now realized would happen in its own time. There was a sense of freedom in this realization.

"I suppose I am the cause of everything bad in the world?" I did not say this sarcastically. I really was beginning to see that I caused everything.

"Let's just say for now that you are the cause of everything bad in *your* world," Ray answered. "But keep in mind that this is nothing but an interim position. One day soon, perhaps, you will begin to see through the illusion of good and bad. You will then begin to embrace the perfect peace of what is. The external world, Charles, is nothing more than a reflection of what is going on inside of you."

"The external world is prison, Ray."

Ray simply stared at me saying nothing. It was then that the realization of what he was trying to tell me came clear. My external world was a violent prison, a reflection of the internal violent prison I had created for myself. My world had become that which I felt inside. Everything around me was an external manifestation of that which I began to feel that day, long ago, when I caught my wife in my bed with another man. I suddenly realized that if I wanted to know what I was feeling inside, all I had to do is look at what was going on around me.

"I would like to ask you something very personal, Charles, if I may."

The muscles in my neck and shoulders tensed slightly as they always do when someone prefaces a question in this way. There was something slightly threatening about it. "Ask," I said in resignation.

"Do you believe in God, Charles?"

"Wow! That's one hell of a question," I thought, and right after thinking it, I said it.

"It's just a question, Charles," Ray replied. "Don't make it into more than it is."

"I don't know how to answer that," I said. "I'd like to believe there is a God, but truthfully, I don't see much evidence for such a thing."

Ray smiled.

"Do you believe in God, Ray?" I asked.

"That depends," Ray answered. "But before I answer that, I want to ask you another question. Can you tell me who or what you are?"

"What do you mean?"

"Well, your entire life you have lived with this sense of self. You have believed in this thing you call your 'self.' From your earliest memories right up to this day, you have believed that this self has been experiencing all of the events in your life. It feels to you like a constant presence that has always been there, and the things that happened in life have been happening to it. I want to know what 'it' is."

"I don't understand the question," I replied. "You're talking about me. I mean, I'm the one who has been experiencing my life."

"Yes, but when you say, 'You're talking about me,' I want to know what this thing you call 'me' is."

"I don't know how to tell you what it is," I protested. "It's just me."

"Don't you find that strange?" Ray asked.

"Find what strange?"

"If I ask you what an apple is, you would tell me it is a fruit that grows on a tree. It is edible, usually red, and it tastes sweet or sometimes tart. You would have no trouble telling me what an apple is. If I ask you what a bed is, you could tell me, or a pillow, or a light bulb, or a tree or a cloud. But let me ask you what this thing to which you refer to as, 'you,' is, and suddenly you are at a total loss for words."

"Ok," I said slowly. "Well then, what do you mean when *you* say 'me'?"

Ray's eyes grew wide with excitement. I had never seen this in him before. "Good question, Charles!" he said. "I have spent a great deal of time trying to figure that out and I have never been able to do so."

"But you're you," I said.

"Am I?" he asked. "I'm not so sure." Ray leaned forward on his bunk, his eyes narrowed and his voice softened. "To tell you the truth, Charles, I'm not so sure there really is a me. I'm beginning to think it is all just a fantasy."

"What do you mean?" I asked.

"I've tried, Charles, I've really tried to find something tangible behind this concept of self, and I can't do it. I've asked myself, 'Am I my body?' I thought perhaps I was. But then if you amputate my leg, do I lose a part of me? No. That wouldn't change this thing I call me at all. I would just become me with one leg. Then I asked, 'Am I my thoughts?' But there is this sense of a me thinking the thoughts. I believe the self to be the thing thinking the thoughts, therefore the self cannot be the actual thoughts. 'Am I my emotions?' The same thing happens when I ask this. Who or what is the 'me' feeling those emotions? 'Am I my brain?' This seemed closer to the truth of the matter, because destroy my brain and I go with it. But did you notice what I just said? I said, 'Destroy *my* brain and *I* go with it.' You see? Even in that sentence, I speak of a 'me' that has a brain, and I speak of an

'I' that will cease to exist if the brain dies. What is this 'me,' or 'I'?"

"I don't know," I answered. "I never thought about it."

"Exactly," Ray said. "No one ever seems to think about that. And yet, look at how we spend our lives. What do you spend every waking moment of your life doing each day?"

"I don't know, breathing," I said.

Ray cocked his head to the side, widened his eyes, and looked at me as if I were an idiot. "I'm serious, Charles," he said.

"Well, I don't know then. You tell me."

"You spend every waking moment of your life serving the wants, the needs, and the desires of this thing you call the 'self.' You are its slave. It is as if you exist for its sake. And yet, you cannot even tell me what 'it' is."

I was beginning to think my head would pop.

"What if it doesn't exist, Charles? What if it is not even real? You have said that you are beginning to realize that you are the cause of all of your troubles, that you have some part in every bad thing that happens to you. Remember saying that?"

"Well, sure I do," I replied.

"Then think about it for a moment. Maybe the reason we cannot define what the self is, is because there really is no such thing as a self. If that is the case, then this 'you' that is causing all of your troubles doesn't even exist. Wouldn't that mean that your troubles don't exist either? Think Charles. Maybe we've got it all wrong. We keep trying to solve all of our so-called 'troubles.' Maybe what we should really try to solve is this so-called 'self.'"

"You've lost me there, Ray," I replied.

Ray paused to consider his next words. "Do you know what nihilism is?" he asked.

"No, what is it?"

"Nihilism is the belief that nothing matters. Nihilists believe that we are nothing more than a particular arrangement of organic matter. To them there is no meaning, no purpose, no great reason for anything. You're born, you live, then you die and that's it."

"Hmmm..." I replied. "They may be onto something there."

"Yes, I think they are," Ray said. "But nihilism is usually thought of as something negative. I mean, nihilists think that, since life has no meaning, and is just a temporary thing that ends in death, the desire to continue living is patently absurd. It makes no sense to continue with the suffering of life when nothing matters anyway."

I thought about that for a moment. "I hate to admit it, Ray, but that makes perfect sense to me."

"It does," Ray replied. "If you believe that you are nothing but one particular arrangement of particulate matter that happens to be self-aware, and if you believe that any attempt to assign meaning to this existence is just your silly little molecules believing they are somehow more than what they really are, then continuing to suffer through a painful life doesn't make sense."

"Well," I said. "Then we just need to kill ourselves. Problem solved." I smiled at Ray, quite proud of my conclusion.

"I agree," Ray said. "That's why I think nihilists are dishonest. I mean, every day they continue to go on living, is another day they do exactly that which stands in opposition to what they profess to believe."

I laughed.

"But what if," Ray continued, "what if the nihilists are basically right? What if nothing that ever happens has any meaning at all? What if it is just stuff happening?"

"Well, Ray, I'll say it again. We should just kill ourselves and be done with it. Peaceful sleep forever as opposed to continued suffering. Seems a simple choice to me."

"Isn't it strange that that is exactly where the human mind is tempted to go? Take away the meaning from life, and he no longer sees any reason to go on living. Is that really the only alternative?"

"It's the only one I can see."

"Couldn't we see it in the opposite way? If life has no meaning and no purpose, couldn't we then just surrender to it and go along for the ride? Think about that. It's not really life that I am attempting to assign meaning to, it is *me* that I am attempting to assign meaning to. What I am really saying is that if *I* don't have any meaning, then *I* don't want to go on living. After all, I don't kill life, it keeps going. I only ponder the idea of killing me. The entire concept of meaning is something I am trying to impose on life, because I want to feel as if I am somehow important. What if I embrace a form of optimistic nihilism in which nothing ever matters, it is all just life doing what life does, and I am a part of it? Couldn't I then just go along for the ride? Wouldn't the experience alone be enough?"

"So…you're saying that there is no meaning to anything. It's just life doing what life does, and we are all a part of it. It's kind of like a movie then. I can enjoy the experience of the movie without having to find any personal meaning in it?"

"Yes, that's exactly what I am saying. A thing does not have to have meaning to be beautiful. A mountain is beautiful, but it doesn't mean anything. Life is beautiful, exactly as it is. We determine that it must have meaning, then we decide to be miserable when we are unable to find meaning in it. Optimistic nihilism is a great reason to go on living. You stop trying to figure things out and start instead allowing things to be as they are. It's all just a ride."

"God damned, Ray," I said laughing. "You're one crazy son-of-a-bitch."

Ray laughed. "But it makes sense, doesn't it?' he asked.

"Yeah, Ray. It does. It's like all that other weird shit you talk about. It all makes sense in a crazy Ray sort of way."

"It's something to think about, anyway."

"That it is, Ray. That it is."

CHAPTER ELEVEN

Any man may easily do harm, but not every man can do good to another.
– Plato

As I have said before, life has an intelligence of its own. Where it once appeared to be totally random, it now seemed as if life had a purpose. It is a funny thing if you stop to think about it. Life seems to know just what you need to learn next, then it does whatever is necessary so you can learn it. This is what life did to me the very next day.

I had just picked up my tray in the chow hall and was about to sit down when a young kid, probably no more than twenty years old, jumped into my seat ahead of me. This kid was a fish and did not understand what such an act meant. He looked at me with a stupid smile that caused a surge of anger to flood my body. I knew what such an act meant, and I knew that the rules of prison required that I do something about it. This kid punked me, and everyone saw it. I wanted to beat the shit out of him right then and there, but guards were everywhere, so I let it pass.

"You gonna let him do you that way?" one of the inmates said as I took another seat.

"The guards are right there," I said. "I'll handle it later."

"He treated you like a little bitch," the man replied.

I gave him my serial killer look that said without saying, "This is none of your fucking business. Stay out of it or you will have an issue with me you aren't going to want."

"It's ok, man," he said. "You handle it your own way. It's no concern of mine."

That was his way of letting me know he realized his mistake and wanted no trouble from me. I said nothing, which was my way of saying "No problem, let's drop it." Prison conversations are funny that way.

By the time I returned to the cell for count I was seething with anger. "I don't know who that punk-assed bitch thinks he is, Ray, but no one treats me like that."

Ray looked up from his book saying nothing.

"I'm gonna fuck him up," I continued.

Ray closed his book and laid it on the bunk beside him. "Why?" he asked.

"Why what?"

"Why are you gonna fuck him up?"

"The little fucker punked me. He's gotta pay," I replied.

"Why don't you just sit down and breathe for a minute?" Ray asked.

"I've got business to handle, Ray," I protested.

"That business can be handled anytime," Ray said. "You go off half cocked and you're gonna get yourself in trouble. Let's just take a minute and calm your ass down."

This made sense to me. I wanted to handle matters, but I didn't want to catch new charges. Perhaps taking a minute to think would be a wise approach.

"Now tell me what happened," Ray said.

I proceeded to give Ray the rundown of the events that transpired.

"Ok," Ray said. "Let's talk about this. Are you breathing?"

I wasn't. My body was too tense.

"Take some deep breaths," Ray instructed. "Let your anger leave you with each exhalation."

I did as he instructed, and soon I felt my anger lessening.

"Good," Ray said. "That's better. Now, this new kid, he got here when? Yesterday?"

"I think so," I said.

"He's never been to prison before, has he? So he doesn't really understand what he did?"

"So?" I asked indignantly.

"*So*, Charles, I want to know why you feel the need to beat him up."

I stared at Ray, stunned. He knew the answer to that question. "Everyone saw what happened. If I don't do something, people will think they can punk my sorry ass."

"Ok," Ray said. "So you're not so worried about the kid. You're concerned with what the other inmates will think if you don't address this situation?"

"Exactly," I said. I was irritated that he would even ask such a thing.

"So what you are doing right now is reacting to fear."

"What!" I shouted as my blood boiled. "I'm not afraid of that fucking kid. I'll beat the brakes off of him."

"Calm down, Charles. Breathe again. I'm on your side here, but you must hear me out. I'm not saying you're afraid of the kid. I'm saying you're afraid of what the other inmates might do if you fail to beat this kid up."

"I wouldn't say I'm afraid," I replied. "Concerned, maybe."

"It doesn't matter what word we use, Charles," Ray continued. "Concern, worry, apprehension, anxiety, all of these words are just various forms of fear. Fear is the constant thread. Fear manifests as worry, doubt, apprehension, etc. You fear that if you don't do something, you will be seen as weak and someone will think they can get away with doing something to you, yes?"

"I'm *concerned* about that, yes."

"Charles."

"Ok! Yes, I am afraid of that."

"Thank you," Ray replied emphatically. "Now let me ask you, had the exact same thing happened, but there was no one there to see it, would you still feel like beating up this kid?"

This may seem like a silly question, but it had the effect of stopping my racing mind in its tracks. My anger also screeched to a halt. Here I was mad at this kid, wanting to beat him up, when in fact, this kid was nothing but a prop. His actions precipitated an event that caused a reaction in me in the form of fear—the fear that the other inmates might now do me harm. I put his face on that fear, and felt the overwhelming desire to attack him. Without realizing it, I saw this kid as the cause of the problem, and I sought the resolution to the problem outside of myself in the form of beating up this young man.

"You're right, Ray," I replied. "If no one were watching, I might have gotten irritated, but I wouldn't want to fight."

"I know that, Charles," Ray said. "I've gotten to know you pretty well, and I'll tell you what you would have done if no one was watching. You would have first felt a touch of irritation, it's true, but you would then have felt concern for the kid. You would have sat with him and explained to him how prison rules worked. You would have warned him that, in prison, doing what he did could get him hurt. You would have sought to help him rather than hurt him."

"That's exactly what I would have done," I answered.

"Yes it is," Ray replied. "That response would be in keeping with your true self. Beating up the kid is born of your false self, the non-existent one, your ego. That self is a purely conditioned self. It believes it exists as a function of your environment, reinforced by your memories. It is telling you that great harm will befall you unless you protect it. That self isn't even real, Charles. It is nothing but conditioned memories, thoughts, a construct of your mind that believes it is something other than your true self. Why don't you go talk to the kid? Explain to him how such actions could get him hurt. Wouldn't *that* be more in keeping with who you are, with who you want to be?"

"What if someone else sees that as weak and then starts something?" I asked.

"Then you will deal with that when, *and if*, it happens. At least that way you will be dealing *with* evil, whereas the way you were tempted to act would be a propagation *of* evil. It is your choice, Charles. Do you want to be what this prison seeks to turn you into? Do you want to be an evil convict who beats up a kid who would be better served by compassion? Think about it, Charles. If you're going to do that, why not go all the way? Why not make the kid your little bitch? Fuck him and then pimp him out to the other inmates. Make him suck cock in exchange for canteen items paid to you. Is that the man you are, Charles? Is that the man you want to be? You have an opportunity here to help that kid. Hell, you may even be able to prevent him from suffering such indignities from someone else. Or you can remain a slave to your ego, and sacrifice that kid at your ego's alter. I think perhaps you do believe in a God, Charles. The God you worship is your ego."

"You didn't have to take it that far, Ray," I protested.

"Yes I did," he replied sternly. This was the first time I ever saw Ray get upset. He recovered quickly.

"The difference between beating him up and raping him is only a matter of degree," he continued. "It's the exact same transgression. One just carries it farther than the other. If you want to be evil, go all out. Don't just go part way so you can convince yourself that you are somehow good. If you want to sacrifice that kid to your pitiful little ego, go ahead. Pimp him out.

Make him your little bitch. Ruin him so that you can feel safe, and so that everyone will know not to fuck with you."

I could think of nothing to say, because there was nothing I could say. Ray was absolutely right. My ego was my God. My entire life was spent in the service of its wants, its needs, its desires. And what a fickle God it was; incessant demands that were forever shifting, always demanding more—more money, more material things, more of whatever made it feel good at the moment. It was like a two-year-old child, forever demanding, never satisfied. I had absolute faith in my ego, even though there was no more evidence for its existence than there was for any other God.

I came face to face that day with the horror of what I had become. I was confronted with a young man who was deserving of my compassion and my understanding, and all I could think of was how this kid was impacting *me*. I was completely and totally self-absorbed. I had no sense of my responsibility to anyone other than me. I was seeking to inflict violence upon another human being. *Seeking* it. I wasn't out to defend myself. I was rationalizing and justifying doing harm to this kid because he did something to threaten my ego self. It was nearly too painful to bear, the thought that I had sunk to this.

"Ah," Ray said, noticing the torment in my eyes. "You are beginning to see exactly what it is you've become. Painful, isn't it?"

"I don't like it, Ray."

"Of course you don't. But you have been blind to it until now so there was nothing you could do to change it. In the old days, they called this demon possession. It is as if something other than you has taken you over. There are no demons, really. It is just conditioned responses driving your behavior, reinforcing ego to the extent that you are now ready to go inflict terrible violence upon an undeserving victim. Now that you see it, it will lose its power. Now you actually have a choice. You no longer have to be driven blindly along. That is freedom from bondage, Charles. That is the path to true peace."

"I need to help that kid, don't I?"

"Yes, you do, Charles." Ray's voice took on a level of compassion I had never before heard from any man.

"And what about the cost to me?"

"There is no cost to you, Charles, because there is no you. That's why the ancient mystics all said, '*Love your brother as yourself.*' They understood, your brother *is* yourself, your brother is you."

I gave birth to something that day. It was tender, young, fragile, and yet unbelievably strong. It would require a great deal of nurturing, but it would grow. It was the virgin birth of the divine child made manifest in me.

• • •

I did speak to the young man. What I learned that day was the extent to which life acts according to my expectations. It is a contradiction. I cannot control or influence life at all, and yet, it acts in response to what I do. Life is a reflection of what is inside of me. I made the determination that day to remain true to who and what I am. The fear that tempted me to act violently was the fear of reprisal from other inmates. Yet this did not happen. There was no reprisal. No one cared. In fact, the few who did take note of what I had done respected my approach. This is a very important point I am making here. Prison changed for me on that day. I should have become everyone's little bitch, but I didn't.

I began to see something I had never seen before. By reacting to my environment, I was allowing my environment to define me. This was not something specific to prison. This was something I had done my entire life. It was how I had lived my life. It took the extreme example of prison to make me see. Prison didn't change, I changed. And when I did, even the violent world of prison began to respond.

I was now beginning to see life as an interaction. It responded to what I did in ways I never realized before. I had heard a quote once, "If you don't eat life, life will eat you." This made sense to me now. In my fear driven existence, all I saw around me was violence. But now, even though the violence of prison still existed, it no longer existed for *me*. The people consumed with that concept saw only one another; I was becoming invisible to them. And suddenly I saw people in prison I had never noticed before. I began to see the men who were not a part of the violence. It was a strange and surreal experience. It seemed as if life was expressing back to me whatever I expressed to it. Life was an exterior expression of my inner self. It was changing in response to the changes in me.

"You're beginning to see things differently now, aren't you?" Ray said to me one evening.

"I believe I am, Ray," I replied.

"Have you thought about the question I asked you a while back?"

"What question is that?"

"Do you believe in God?"

"I've thought about it."

"And?"

"I find it difficult to believe in God, Ray," I replied. "I would like to believe God exists, but I cannot get past the fact that there is no evidence of such a thing. It seems to me that God is something man invented to comfort himself."

"You may be right," Ray said.

"What do you mean?" I asked.

"It doesn't matter if God exists or not," he said. "The belief in God is comforting, and, it works. People are comforted, and that in itself is a good thing."

"You were going to tell me what you thought about God," I said.

"Yes I was. And I think you are ready to hear it now," Ray replied. He sat up on his bunk, drew his knees to his chest and let out a deep breath. "God is a funny subject," he said. "I think all people have to come to their own conclusions about it. My understanding of God was directly tied to my understanding of self."

"Really?" I replied.

Ray smiled. "There was a time," he continued, "when I thought of my skin as a boundary. Everything inside my skin was me. Everything outside my skin was other than me. Then one day I read about Aspen trees."

"Aspen trees?" I asked. This was typical of Ray. Somehow trees taught him something new. Everything seemed to teach Ray something new.

"Yeah, Aspen trees," He said. "Aspen trees live in groves containing many individual trees. But underneath the ground, these Aspen trees share a common root system. They experience life as individual trees, and yet, they are actually one single organism."

"Really?" I said.

"It's true," Ray replied. "And when I read that, it dawned on me that people are not that different. Perhaps we too experience life as separate individuals even though we are really one organism. I was struck with the idea that I cannot do harm to another human being without actually doing harm to myself. I mean, the harm I once did to another human being put me in prison. The harm you were about to inflict on that kid would have done far more harm to you than it would ever have done to him. This concept seems to be universal. The Aspen trees helped me make sense of this. If I am one Aspen tree, and you are another, if someone poisons you *I* will get sick."

I thought about this and somehow it was making sense.

"And then I thought," Ray continued, "that if I am one Aspen tree and you are another, I cannot harm you without harming me because we are really one. In fact, in order to do harm to you, I first have to convince myself that I am somehow *other* than you. Only by maintaining that illusion can I then inflict harm. And yet, maintaining that illusion changes nothing. Harming you *does* do great harm to me. I don't think we humans are all that different from Aspen trees. I think we are all individual expressions of a single organism, if you will. And that single organism is what people refer to when they speak of God."

I furrowed my brow. "But I thought God was a man-like being who lived in Heaven," I replied.

"I think that depiction is a metaphor for what I am saying," Ray answered. "We humans cannot conceive of the infinite expression known as God, so we think of him as an individual. To me, God is more of an intelligent, animating energy expressing itself through all things. When I abandoned the idea of a personal, man-like God, and began instead to see God as an energy expression, things began to fall into place. God isn't a man, God is an expression. Life itself is that expression we know as God. Life has an intelligence to it. And when we surrender our ego selves to that intelligence, we find our true place and our true purpose."

"And what is that purpose?" I asked.

"To give to others," Ray replied. "I've used my time in prison to read and to study these matters. My life had gone so badly that my entire belief system was shaken to the core. I began to study all the different religions, but I sought what was common to them as opposed to what was different. I found that all the ancient mystics spoke to this same truth. We spend our lives trapped in the prison of the ego self. That self thinks that it can wrest satisfaction out of life. Toward that end, it is always seeking more. It exists, believing in the fantasy that more of something will make it happy. *'If I could just get more money, more material possessions, more drugs, more women, more anything, then I will be content.'* But it never works. More of anything is at best a temporary solution. It feels good, but it never really satisfies. You end up feeling like there is a void at the center of your being that can never be filled. You forever seek to fill it with more of something, anything. But no matter how much you feed the beast, it always wants more. Soon life begins to feel like a meaningless struggle to get more. And nothing you do will ever quiet the hunger. I cannot satisfy me.

"Yet when you turn that around, when you stop seeking to feed yourself and you start seeking instead to comfort others, that void begins to dissipate. That is the common thread that runs through all religions. Only by doing for you can I fill the emptiness in me. The Chinese have a book called the *Tao te Ching* in which it is said, 'See the world as yourself.' The Buddha said, 'See others as yourself.' Even Jesus said to love your brother as yourself. They are all speaking to this same realization. I read a prayer by Saint Francis once in which he said, 'Lord help that I might seek to comfort rather than be comforted, understand rather than be understood, love rather than be loved. *For it is through self forgetting that one finds.*' They all say the same thing. My true expression is not to be realized in service to my ego self. It is only to be realized through service to others. You and I are one."

I was struck dumb by these words. Didn't I just experience exactly this that Ray was speaking about? I chose to comfort the young man who I thought offended me. And through comforting him, my world changed. "So…" I began, "we should seek then to live the godly life?"

"Forget the godly life," Ray replied.

This surprised me. "But I thought…"

"Stop thinking," Ray insisted. "Trying to live the godly life is just your ego trying to take over again. It will try to assert its control in a new way so you become the keeper of the truth, and everything you do will be done ultimately to make you feel better. That is just a form of selfish altruism and it is meaningless. It is doing for others only because of what it does for you. That inflates the ego, and pretty soon you're out trying to save the world. That's what the prison chaplain does, and you know how you felt when speaking to him."

"Well then, what should I do?" I asked.

"Get your ego out of the way and start allowing this thing we call God to live *your* life. That makes all the difference. There is no longer anything in it for you, because there is no longer a *you* invested in it. To serve God, you must see God as the expression manifesting in all living things and then you serve *them*."

"What if I don't believe in God?" I asked.

"You don't have to believe in God," Ray replied.

"I don't understand, Ray."

"Stop telling yourself that you must first determine that God is real before you believe. You will never be able to prove God is real. And whether God is real or not doesn't matter. What is real is people's belief in God. And if you are really honest, you will find that people who believe are able to get through difficulties in life that would utterly destroy you."

"So you are telling me to believe in something that may not be there?"

"Exactly," Ray answered. "Stop trying to prove to yourself why such thinking works and simply accept *that* it works. Absolute surrender of the self, and a life devoted to the service of others leads to peace. A life spent trying to serve your own needs does not. It is that simple; you need not think about it beyond that. You just have to live it and then you will see. There was a Danish philosopher named Sören Kierkegaard who spoke of an irrational leap of faith. He said we all have this urge toward the divine, even though there is no rational, logical proof for the existence *of* the divine. The leap into faith cannot be based on logic. Looking forward, there is no empirical evidence in support of such a decision. But after we make that leap and we look back, we then are able to see it as supremely rational. We then see this thing we call God in everything. The rewards of doing this are profound. I cannot tell you *why* this works. I cannot tell you *how* this works. I can only tell you *that* it works."

I listened intently to what Ray was telling me, and as I did, I noticed a disturbance in my soul. I wanted to reject this idea of God and think of it as I always had—silly superstition. Had anyone other than Ray said this to me, I would have rejected it as such. But here before me sat a man for whom these concepts were working in his life. This was a fact I could not deny. In the depths of prison, one of the darkest places on earth, this man had found something that had forever eluded me. And it was this fact that gave his words force. He had seen something I had not. And even though I was not ready to accept the existence of a God, I was willing to keep my mind open to the possibility that there was something to what Ray was telling me.

Charles Bynum

CHAPTER TWELVE

The path into the dark appears light. –The Tao te Ching

Human beings tend to like things simple. Something is either on or off, up or down, simple or difficult...good or bad. But life is not like that. Life refuses to conform to our silly little expectations. Even so, we are loathe to admit it; to see life as it really is. We try to force it to fit what we think it ought to be, and when it doesn't conform, well, that's when things become difficult for us. We want everything in neat little categories, yet even our very selves do not fit such categories. For instance, am I good, or am I bad? That is a difficult question to answer. Everyone in prison believes himself to be basically good—they just made a mistake or did one thing that was bad, according to them. But when I look deeply into myself, the only honest answer to that question is...yes.

I struggled with this at times. I, like everyone else in prison, thought myself basically good—I just did a few bad things when life treated me unfairly. I then wanted to climb on my soapbox and shout, "How dare anyone judge me; you'd have done the same thing if you were in my position." And that is what we do. We compare our sins to those of others, then determine the others to be evil, while absolving ourselves as good. We think we understand why we did what we did, and with that understanding, we judge our sins to be less severe than the sins of other people, therefore, we are basically good. But I wonder, do we ever really understand why we do anything? We build elaborate stories after the fact, to be sure, but if we look at any difficult time in our lives, won't we find that we were driven blindly along by some sinister force that seemed at times to be outside ourselves? We feel carried along by emotion, as if we could do no other than what we did, and yet, we are still fully responsible. The tidal wave of emotion drives us inexorably toward a choice that, at the time, feels like no choice at all. It is only afterward that it feels like a choice. When it is happening, one feels more like a character in a movie being driven along by fate.

Am I a good man? This question takes on new meaning in prison. I can be a good man; I have been a good man. Most of the things I did throughout my life were good. But there was always that "other" acting through me as well. That selfish something that often did mean things to those around me. Am I an evil man because of the few bad things I did? Do these outweigh all the good things I have done? I suppose the question I was beginning to ask was, "Who am I?" And the more I asked, the more I found that I hadn't the slightest clue.

"May I ask you a personal question Ray?" I asked one evening after lights out.

Ray looked up from his book, "Sure," he answered cautiously.

"I want to know why you're here. I mean, you've been here a long time and you've said you will die here. What did you do that brought you here?"

There is an unspoken rule in prison; you never ask a man what his crime was. The only exception to that rule was your cell-mate.

The idea was that if you live that closely with a man, you have a right to know.

Ray laid his book down and stared hard at me. He knew the rule as well as I did, but he still seemed reluctant to answer.

"Why do you want to know?" he asked.

"Because you don't seem to belong here," I answered. "You are clearly a well-educated, highly intelligent man. You're not like the other men in the prison. It just doesn't make sense that you would be in here for the rest of your life. I can't figure out why a man like you would end up spending his life in prison."

His penetrating glare cut deeply into me. He was studying me, attempting to determine if I was sincere. I was.

"You are correct," he said. "I have a college degree and I worked as an engineer before I got myself into trouble." He sat up in his bunk. "I will tell you what you want to know," he continued, "but I don't want it repeated. This is between you and me."

I nodded in agreement.

"My wife called me at my office one day to ask me to pick up our thirteen-year-old daughter at the bowling alley on my way home from work. She had apparently spent the afternoon there with friends, and as it was on my route home, I agreed to stop and get her. My wife said my daughter would be waiting out front, but when I got there, she was nowhere to be found. I parked the car and went inside, but I still couldn't find her. I couldn't find her friends either. I later learned that they had walked across the street to the mall and left my daughter to wait for me. But she wasn't there. I began walking around the parking lot, still no sign of her. I heard a commotion in the back of the bowling alley and I went to see what it was. That's when I saw her. She was lying on the ground, beaten, bloody, and screaming, fighting against a young man who was on top of her. "

Ray paused a moment as he replayed the memory of that day in his mind.

"I don't know what happened. I went absolutely insane. I ran to her, and the young man jumped up as I approached. There was a look of terror in his eyes and he was saying 'No…no,' but there was no stopping me. I pounced on him. I began beating him with a fury and a madness I never knew myself to possess. I beat him and beat him, and then I put my hands around his throat and strangled the life out of him. I even bit a hunk of flesh out of his face. I was like a wild animal, completely out of control."

I thought for a moment. "But Ray," I said, "wouldn't that be justifiable homicide?"

"Technically, no," he answered. "The law only allows you to use whatever force is necessary to remove the threat. Once he was beaten and unconscious, he was no longer a threat. To kill him then was murder."

"But that would still be manslaughter," I protested. "They wouldn't give you a life sentence for that."

Ray put his hands up, palms facing the floor. "Hang on Charles, you're getting ahead of me here. Let me finish my story."

"Okay, I'm sorry," I said.

Ray took in a deep breath and let it out slowly. "It turns out," he continued, "that the young man I killed was not her attacker at all. He was a seventeen-year-old high school kid who worked at the bowling alley. He was taking out some garbage when he surprised the man who *was* trying to rape my daughter. The man apparently took off running when he saw the kid. This young man was trying to help my daughter. But she was so traumatized that she was struggling against him, so, when I came around the corner it looked to me like he was attacking her. He wasn't. He prevented my little girl from being raped…and I killed him."

A tear formed in the corner of his eye. I sat stunned, not knowing what to say.

"I'll never forget that look of terror in his eyes when I came upon him," Ray continued. "He tried to tell me that it wasn't him, but I couldn't hear. I'll also never forget his mother when she arrived at the scene. I was in the back of a patrol car watching as she screamed and wretched inconsolably over the loss of her child. In that one instant, everything changed. And I caused it."

Tears were flowing from both his eyes now and he wiped them away with the bottom of his tee-shirt.

"Anyway," he said, "they gave me six years for manslaughter. So, off to prison I went. I figured with parole I would be out in four. I kept to myself and tried to stay out of trouble. About a year into my stretch, a young kid decided that he would give me grief. He was calling me out in the yard. People told me that if I didn't handle my business, everyone would be punking me before long. So I went to his cell and fought him. During the fight he fell, hit his temple on the corner of a metal bookshelf, one just like that one there. It killed him instantly. Freak thing, you know, but he was dead just the same. If I had fought him in my cell, I could have claimed self-defense, but as I was in his, the DA charged me with premeditated murder. I couldn't afford an attorney, so I got a public defender who was inept and who didn't care at all about defending a murderer against yet another charge of murder. The DA portrayed me as a man who liked killing young men. So, here I am. Life without parole."

"My God, Ray. I don't know what to say."

"Don't say anything. Learn from it. Think about what happened to me the next time you go half-cocked into someone's cell. Let me tell you something Charles. Getting out of prison is harder than you think. Anything could go wrong at any time, and you'll be here forever."

I thought about the time Ray pulled me off that man who I was attacking in his cell. Had Ray not done that, I might have suffered the same fate as he. "Do you still see your daughter?" I asked.

"She writes me sometimes," Ray answered. "But she lives too far away to visit."

"So you were basically just someone with really bad luck?" I asked.

Ray stared at me. He had that look I had seen many times before, contemplating his next words. I had learned that this meant something important was about to be said. "No, Charles," he said. "I was not someone suffering from a run of bad luck." Ray smiled, stared down at the floor and shook his head. "You know, it's funny," he continued, "everything in me wants to go along with your idea that it was just bad luck. I want to portray myself as a victim of circumstances that were simply beyond my control. I can't do that, Charles. That's the kind of shit that got me put in here."

"What do you mean?" I asked.

"The truth is, I was always a hot-tempered son-of-a-bitch," he said. "I was always popping off at my wife and daughter, and I wasn't above slapping them now and then if I thought they deserved it. That's the truth about how I was. I never bothered to take any responsibility for it at all. My motto was 'I wouldn't lose my temper if you would act right.' It was always someone else's fault that I acted like I did, just like I'm tempted to let you believe that it was not my fault I killed that kid. I was ashamed of who I was, Charles. And that shame prevented me from looking at myself *as* I was. Instead, I maintained an image of myself as better than I knew myself to really be. And because of that, I kept on being exactly what I was, while lying myself into believing I wasn't."

As Ray spoke, I found myself becoming increasingly uncomfortable. His words were hitting a bit too close to home.

"Here is the other part of the story, Charles, the part I don't like to admit. I had a tendency to drink too much, and I had picked up a pint on my way to the bowling alley that evening. Alcohol only served to make my temper worse. I had nearly finished the bottle by the time I arrived, and I was madder than hell that I couldn't find my daughter. I was in a near rage *before* I found her. That kid was trying to tell me that he was not her attacker, and somewhere in me I can't help but to think that I knew this at the time, but my alcohol-fueled rage had me. I gave myself over to the anger and I killed him."

Ray leaned back in his bunk and sighed heavily. "My wife and my daughter were always afraid of me, Charles. They were afraid of my drinking, and they were afraid of my temper. That is the simple fact that I could never face. And because I could never face it, other people suffered. Other people paid the price for my failure. That kid lost his life. His mother lost her son. My wife lost her husband, and my daughter lost her father. All of that happened because I was too cowardly to look honestly at myself—too filled with shame to be able to look at myself as I really was. My failure caused a lot of people a lot of suffering.

"And the truth be told, it was that same anger that killed that kid in prison. It's still hard for me to tell it like it really was. That which I said before is bullshit. Well, it's not exactly bullshit. I *was* worried about him punking me, and about what the other inmates would think. But more than that, I was just plain angry. I wanted to kill him and I did. I was a very bad man, Charles, and I deserve what I got."

I stared at Ray, stunned. Never before had I seen anyone take such full responsibility for his own failures. I was struck to the core with my inability to take responsibility for my own.

"I did something very similar, Ray," I said.

"Oh? How's that?"

"When my marriage failed, all I could do was see myself as a victim. I could only see how unfair it all was to *me*. I turned to drugs to cope and…" my voice cracked. I fought back the tears. My body wretched in agony. "My poor little girl," I said and I looked up at Ray through tear-filled eyes. "She needed me to be there for her, and I wasn't. I abandoned her when she needed me most. I was a sorry excuse for a father; a sorry excuse for a man. I don't know how to live with that, Ray. I can't reconcile my behavior with who I want to believe myself to be. I hate…" Words left me. The tears flowed harder.

"You hate what, Charles?" Ray asked.

"I…I hate me, alright!" I snapped. "I fucking hate me! I can't stand me! What kind of man could do such a thing? God Damn it!" I was sobbing now. I had, at long last, given voice to the demon that consumed me. Ray walked to my bunk, sat beside me, and placed his hand on my shoulder.

"It's okay, Charles," he said softly. "Now that you've said it, you will find that from this moment onward you have a choice. You no longer have to be that man that you hate. Now you can begin to heal."

"I don't want to heal. I don't deserve to heal."

"None of us deserve to heal, Charles. That's the human condition. If there is a God, none of us deserve his forgiveness. That's what the concept of grace is all about. We don't deserve forgiveness, yet we are given it just the same. If we surrender ourselves to it, we can begin to heal."

"But I don't believe there is a God," I replied.

"You don't have to believe it, Charles. Just surrender yourself to it. Stop thinking. Stop trying to make sense of it all. Just let it take you wherever it will. Let go, Charles."

War raged in my soul. I wanted to let go of it, to accept it fully and be free of it. I also feared letting go of it. Who was I without it? Who was I without my self-hate and self-loathing? It then came to me. I created it. I nurtured it. And I was now trying with all my might to hang onto it. I was tired, and it was time. I let go.

Looking back, I realize something that escaped me at the time. Ray had just told me a story that was very painful for him to tell. He fought back tears of guilt and remorse while telling it. And yet, he was looking out for me. He told me his story so that I might learn from it. He told me because he wanted to help me heal from my own suffering. That meant he wasn't angry. A lesser man would have been filled with anger and hate for a system that had done this to him. But Ray was not a lesser man. Ray was a man who accepted full responsibility for what he had done, and through that acceptance, became the strongest man I had ever known. His greatest weakness had been transformed into his greatest strength. By any definition, that was nothing less than a miracle. Ray's concern was for me, a man he met in a prison cell. He wanted nothing more than for me to heal as he had healed. I had never experienced such kindness before.

Charles Bynum

CHAPTER THIRTEEN

Do not go where the path may lead, go instead where there is no path and leave a trail. – Ralph Waldo Emerson

Prison works on a point system. Your points go up if you receive any disciplinary actions such as write ups for disobeying staff, getting in fights or anything else they can pin on you. If you go six months without a write up, your points drop. Mine had been dropping, and before I knew it, I was called into my case manager's office for a meeting. I was told that my points had dropped enough that I was to be transported to a lower security facility. I would be leaving the following morning. Prison is like that; your life is subject to sudden changes that can occur at any time.

This was good news. The lower security facility meant that I would no longer be in a controlled movement prison. I would have the freedom to walk out onto the yard, go to the library, etc., anytime I wanted without having to wait for that damned buzzer to tell me I could move. On the other hand, it meant having to get situated in a new prison with people I did not know and having to re-establish myself amongst the inmates there. It also meant I would be leaving Ray.

"My points dropped, Ray," I said when I returned to my cell. Ray knew what that meant.

"Congratulations," he said, and yet I could sense in his voice his disappointment that I was leaving. It is very hard to make friends in prison; harder still to lose one. I knew I would never see Ray again. He knew it too. I also felt an inner conflict. I was pleased to be progressing, yet I did not want to show my pleasure because it was rude to do so in front of those left behind. Ray was going to die in prison. There would be no progressions for him, no matter how well he behaved. Seeing me move on was a reminder to him that he never would.

"I am sorry to be leaving you Ray," I said.

"That's nonsense," Ray replied. "It's time for you to be moving on. You will do well; I have no doubt about that."

I hardly slept that night. I was both excited and apprehensive about the new leg of my journey that I was about to embark upon. And I also worried about Ray. Prison is a very impersonal place. Being in prison made me appreciate prisons in a way I never had before. I mean, there are many, many men in prison that I would not want to meet out on the streets. But there were also men like Ray; men who had undergone true changes and no longer resembled the men they once were, the men they were when they were sent to prison. These men were grouped in with all the rest. Because of that, there would be no hope for Ray no matter how well he was doing. The individual is completely devalued in prison. This is a problem, but I don't think greater respect for the individual is the solution. I think it is individuality *itself* that is the problem. Any system that greatly values some individuals is sure to devalue others. I no longer believed society to be a collection of individuals. It was instead an interaction of expressions. Our prisons are a reflection of the failures inherent in those interactions. We like to think that the individuals themselves bear the total burden of responsibility for their situation. But the problem seems to be deeper than that. To me, it was beginning to seem as if systemic problems throughout the collective society were made manifest in the form of the individual prisoner. I'm not saying the individual bears no responsibility, because he is responsible for his actions. I am only saying that it is too easy for society to place the total burden upon him, absolving itself of any and all responsibility for the environment that created the prisoner. We have taken individuality to the extreme, and some people get trampled in the process.

At four o'clock the following morning, a guard woke me to tell me to get ready for transport. I got up and got myself dressed. Ray sat up and watched me as I made myself ready.

"It's been good knowing you," Ray said.

"Are you going to be alright?" I asked.

Ray smiled. "Don't you go worrying about me, Charles. You just keep doing what you're doing and get yourself the hell out of here. I want you to get on with your life."

A wave of sadness flooded over me. "It doesn't seem fair, Ray," I said. "I mean, you being left here and all."

"This is my life now," he replied. "I'm at peace with it. Besides, look what my presence here has done for you, Charles. The older I get, the more things seem to be happening exactly as they are supposed to. Besides, I am more free than most of the people running around in the real world. They don't realize it, but they are prisoners of the mind. Those are the loneliest walls of all."

"But Ray…"

"Time to go." My escort had arrived. I shook Ray's hand, then he drew me in and hugged me tightly.

"Go on, Charles. Make me proud."

I turned and left. I stopped at the door to take one last look at the tiny cell Ray and I had called home. "Goodbye Ray," I said, and I never saw him again.

The guard escorted me and nine others to the transport bus. We waited in line to be placed in full restraints—hands shackled to a chain around the waist, legs shackled together. We boarded the bus and took our seats on hard plastic benches. My new journey had begun.

For twelve hours I rode on that hard, uncomfortable seat with my arms and legs bound. The shackles dug into my ankles making them bleed by the time we finally arrived. The restroom facilities were set up for urinating only. About half way through the trip, the urge to defecate became overwhelmingly painful, but there was nothing I could do. They did not feed us that day. Once again I was reminded of the myriad of small tortures one endures when one is no longer thought of as a human being. Should I forget that the guards did not see me as human, the guard sitting in a locked cage at the back of the bus with a loaded shotgun pointed at my head served as an uncomfortable reminder. I remember looking at that guard, wondering what it must be like to be paid to kill another human being should circumstances warrant it. I wondered, did he want to kill me? Was he sitting there hoping for an excuse to take a human life? But then, I wasn't a human being anymore, was I? I was just some piece of animated flesh in the shape of a man who needed to be transported.

We stopped at a supermax prison along the way to pick up people being progressed out of twenty-three hour a day lockdown. A big, mean looking black man boarded the bus and took the seat next to me. I nodded as he sat; he nodded back. In prison, you have to do some pretty bad things to get sent to a supermax. I didn't know what this guy had done, but I had no doubt he could be dangerous. I decided not to say anything.

After about an hour, he spoke to me. "Been in supermax for ten calendar years," he said. I was shocked. I had been in the hole for forty-five days and it nearly drove me insane. I couldn't imagine what ten years in that hell would be like.

"Really," I replied.

"Yeah," he said. "You the first muth-fucka I spoke to in ten years."

"How did you manage to survive that?" I asked.

"You gotta be strong," he replied. "It's all about keeping yo mind straight. Mutha-fuckas tried to break me, but I was too strong for 'em."

This man was no longer fully human. He was hard in a way only those in prison can become hard. And he was dangerous. A man like this could fly off at any minute, for any reason. And yet, somewhere deep in him, he was still a human being. For ten years he had been deprived of human contact, and for ten years he longed for someone to talk to, someone to listen to him. As fate would have it, I was to be that person.

For the next few hours, I listened to this man speak of his life. I said very little. I sensed that he needed to talk and I thought it best to stay quiet. His name was Joe. He told me of his life before prison, his time in prison, and he spoke of the horror of the last ten years. He reminded me of an animal starved for food; but he was a human being starved for human contact. It occurred to me that he no longer knew how to carry on a normal conversation in which he would listen to the words of another. His past ten years had been a constant one-man dialog with himself. It was that dialog that apparently had saved him. Now he was able to speak that dialog to another. It seemed to be helping him. He was still talking when the bus, at long last, arrived at the holding facility called cell house five.

Prison transport in an interesting science. There are busses coming in from all over the state. These busses stop at numerous prisons along the way, picking up any convicts who are scheduled for transport. Some prisoners, like me, are progressing to lower security facilities. Others are going to higher security places. Some of the more fortunate prisoners are going home.

No matter where you are going, you will first go to cell house five. Cell house five is the holding facility where you stay until the transport out to the facility you are slated to go to is scheduled to leave. You have no idea how long you will be there. The average stay is three days, but some people end up stuck there for three weeks. The layout was a long hallway with three tiers of cells on either side. Once we were safely locked inside, our shackles were removed. We were then given bed rolls and sent to our assigned cells. I was on the second tier; Joe was given a cell on the third tier.

You are only allowed out of the cell to go to chow. They alternate the order so that each tier gets the chance to go to chow first. For breakfast, the first tier goes first, for lunch the second, and for dinner, the third. We arrived just before dinner and Joe's tier went first. As soon as the convicts cleared the facility, my tier was released. I walked to the chow hall and got my tray. I saw Joe sitting alone so I went and sat with him. We spent what little time we had talking. It was a dangerous thing for me to do, and other prisoners warned me that Joe was wound so tight he could pop at any moment. If that happened, I had no doubt he would kill me. And yet I felt like I was doing what I needed to do. I was Joe's first human contact, and being his friend seemed to be the most important thing in the world.

When my tier was called before Joe's, I would wander slowly in the line waiting for him. When Joe was called before me, I would find him in the chow hall and sit with him. By the second day, he was listening to me as I shared some of the events of my life. He was re-learning how to have a normal conversation with another human being. My speaking to him broke all of the prison rules. And by breaking the prison rules, I mean, he was black and I was white. People of different skin-colors are none too trusting of one another in prison. I sensed that Joe wondered what this crazy white boy wanted with him; what was my angle. But I ignored all this and spoke to him as a friend, as a fellow human being. It was the first time I felt life carrying me along, and I was able to feel this because I was surrendering myself to it. It was just as Ray told me it would be. Life, it seems, really does have an intelligence to it. I knew how dangerous this man was, I knew I could be killed by him at any minute for any reason. But I wasn't afraid. I also somehow knew that I was placed there to talk to him, to reach out to him, to aid him in his transition to a more normal existence. I was no longer the center of everything. Instead, I was a very small part of something much larger than me—but I was an important part. I was one thread in the tapestry of life; each and every thread just as important as every other.

By the third day, an amazing thing happened. Joe's tier was called first, and when my tier was finally called, I headed to the chow hall prepared to find him and sit with him as I had previously done. But as I approached the chow hall, I looked up and there was Joe standing at the door. He was waiting for me. It would have brought tears to my eyes had I not been afraid he would have killed me for crying. I simply said, "Hey Joe," and we got in line together to get our trays of food.

I was transported shortly after that. I never saw Joe again. Yet I got the strange sensation that I had done something very important for him. I reached out to him when no one else would, and I did so at a time in his life when he most needed it. I experienced for the first time something else Ray often talked about. He told me how placing other people's needs ahead of my own was the only path to peace. I felt moved to do that for Joe. And I felt that sense of inner peace Ray spoke of. Had I chosen not to do it, not to surrender to life as it nudged me along, I would have missed this experience. Had I allowed my fear of this man, and the advice of others to convince me to stay away, the peace I now felt would never have come to me. Ray was right. It had been there all along. I was unable to see it because I was too far into my head to ever allow myself to do that which would allow me to experience it. The words Ray once quoted to me from the 'Tao te Ching" came to my mind. "You cannot know it, you can only be it." No amount of rational discourse could ever have convinced me such a thing was possible. I had to experience it for myself. It was that irrational leap of faith thing. Before you do it, it makes no sense. After you do it, it makes perfect sense. I didn't know it at the time, but I was beginning to discover my true purpose.

Transport to my new facility was only an hour away and I was thrilled to not have to be on the bus for very long. Upon my arrival, I was escorted to my new cell where I met my new cell mate, James. He seemed likable enough. I unpacked my things, and James offered to show me around.

The first thing he did was show me the day hall. There were tables with men playing cards, dominoes and chess. He then said, "Let's go check out the yard." He walked right past the guard station and out the unit door. I stopped dead in my tracks, afraid to go outside without permission. I turned to the guard. "I can just walk out?" I asked.

"Just come back when the buzzer sounds for count," he said, laughing at me. I was certain I was not the first inmate to ask such a question.

I stepped out the door of my own accord. It was the first time in two years I had done such a thing and there was a thrilling sense of freedom in it.

This was a far nicer facility than the one I had left. There was a quarter-mile jogging track lined with housing units. In the center of the track was the weight pile and handball courts. James took me to the prison library where I was able to check out books. I had a degree of freedom here that I had not known in some time. I was frightened of it, yet elated at the same time. It was still prison, but this place seemed far more bearable.

There was also less violence here. Fights sometimes occurred, but they were rare. The men who made it this far were on their way home, and they didn't want anything to interfere with that. Things would be much better here, I began to think. As it turned out, they were.

Charles Bynum

CHAPTER FOURTEEN

A mind enclosed in language is in prison. – Simone Weil

Adjusting to my new surroundings was very similar to adjusting to the first prison I was sent to. But things were also very different. The other men were sizing me up just as before, but I was no longer consumed with fear; no longer worried about what the men thought. There was a new found sense of confidence growing within me. It was a different feeling from anything I had ever felt before. The environment in which I found myself was not as important. What was important was what was going on inside of me.

Ray often spoke of this. He would tell me that the outer world was but a reflection of what was going on inside of me. He would tell me that we project our reality, that we create it much like we do when dreaming. In a dream, I think that the world around me is real, and I think things are happening to me. But in fact, I am the one dreaming, and the world I see is completely my creation. These were the things Ray would say, and they never made sense to me. But now they were beginning to make sense. The real world might not be all that different from a dream after all. Perhaps Ray was correct and the environment in which I find myself *is* a projection, an interaction with my mind. It was beginning to seem this way to me. As I began to incorporate these changes, my environment changed in response. I was no longer the angry, violent man I had been before, and my experience of prison changed along with the change in me.

The first thing I noticed was that my new cellie, James, was no Ray. He was a miserable soul who felt life had treated him terribly unfairly. He did not assume responsibility for his situation as Ray had done. He blamed all of his woes on a woman. Had it not been for her, his reasoning concluded, he would not be in prison.

"Yeah, that little bitch thought she could get away with that shit," he said to me one day. James was thirty-five years old, had curly black hair and a thick moustache. There was nothing tough or hard about him. He seemed like the guy everyone picked on in high school.

"She took my money then had me kicked out of my home," he continued.

"How'd she get you kicked out of your home?" I asked.

"Bitch called the law on me. Told'em I was beatin on her."

"Were you?" I asked.

"Well, yeah, but she *deserved* it. What kind of woman calls the cops on you? The kind who deserves to be beat, that's what kind of woman. Cop-callin' bitch."

Getting to know James was a wonderful experience for me. And by wonderful, I mean irritating as all hell. But it was good for me too. In him I could see clearly how a person creates his own reality, then projects that reality upon another. James was, in his mind, a perpetual victim. He was utterly blind to the role his own hand played in his life. He could not see that the reality in which he found himself was in fact a reality he had created. James was as I had been.

I also learned how futile it is to try to make someone see this. I tried various ways to get James to assume responsibility for his current condition, to no avail. His resistance was total. He would become irritated with my suggestions. After some time, I determined that it was best to simply listen to him without attempting to make him see anything. But I would often speak of my own situation and my own responsibility in the hope that he might make the connection. He never did. I could see that the lessons I had learned, the lessons Ray had taught me, were only available to those whose eyes were ready to be opened. You cannot save another person; you can only be there to help them when they are ready to save themselves.

It was at this point that I decided I would try meditating. Ray always spoke highly of it. Now that I didn't have Ray to talk to, it seemed a good time to try it. It was also a useful tool to get James to shut up when I grew tired of his rantings. Ray told me once that it is my mind that is the source of all my suffering, and that meditation was basically the practice of observing my mind and learning how it really operated. He said there was much to be discovered by observing one's thoughts. I decided to find out for myself, so I went to the prison library and checked out all the books I could find on meditation.

The result of all my studies was more or less a state of confusion. Some books told me to force my mind to be quiet. Others told me to concentrate on one thought and push all other thoughts out. Some said that chanting words like *"om"* was the proper way to meditate. Others said to count my breaths. But there were a few books that said the proper thing to do was simply observe the mind, watch the thoughts as if I was a third person observing what was going on inside of my head. This seemed the most appropriate thing to me, and it had the added benefit of being the closest to what Ray had told me to do.

Thus began my meditation practice. I would spend every hour I could sitting quietly, watching the activities of my mind.

Actually, in the beginning, I could only spend a few minutes at a time meditating. Thoughts raced through my mind uncontrollably. These racing thoughts caused a sense of agitation to grow in my body. I simply could not sit for long, and I would have to get up and do something to ease my suffering.

I found exercise to be most helpful. I began working out regularly on the weight pile in the yard. This practice seemed to burn off much of the energy in my body, which made meditation easier. I started working out to a point of near exhaustion, then I would return to my cell to meditate. Before long, I was able to sit for longer periods without my body forcing me to get up and move about.

In what seemed like no time at all, I began to see things happening in my mind. I saw that my brain was in a constant state of activity, thought after thought continually popping into my head. I always knew that my mind seemed to be in a perpetual state of chatter, but I never was aware of just how much chatter was going on. I saw that the chatter began the moment I awoke in the morning, and it continued until I fell asleep at night. I was amazed at the degree of mental activity, and at the amount of energy wasted on these numerous thoughts. But try as I might, I could not control these thoughts, nor could I make them stop. I was forever lost in a conversation with myself. And I was surprised at how much of this activity took place without me being aware of it. The more I observed, the more aware I became.

I began to see that all this thinking was interfering with my ability to experience life as it was. Rather than experiencing life as it happened, I was describing life to myself with words. It was a constant monologue that kept me one step removed from life. It was an interesting discovery. I saw that one thought would pop into my head, and before I knew it, another thought would jump in replacing the previous one. I tried to remain present by using some technique such as focusing on my breathing. But in the span of a few seconds, some new thought would come into my mind and I found myself carried away by it, completely forgetting that I was meditating. I tried counting my breaths, but I would forget to count by breath number two, some new and compelling thought having carried me completely away. It was maddening. I was amazed to learn that my mind seemed to have a mind of its own.

The observation of my mind that I practiced in meditation began to spill over into all aspects of my life. Soon I was observing everything as if I were someone else watching my life unfold. It was like watching a movie. I was a character in the drama unfolding around me, nothing more. Sometimes events in life would pull me into the drama. During those times, I was no longer observing, I was completely lost in whatever was going on. But I started noticing when this was happening, and I would go back to observing. Life, it seemed, would trick me into forgetting, and I would find myself reacting to events without any true awareness. Then I would catch myself doing this, return to my observation of life, and suddenly a space would open up. This space allowed me the time to formulate a conscious response as opposed to an utterly unconscious reaction. I began to realize that as long as I was aware and observing, I was in a state of inner peace, no matter what was going on around me. I lost that sense of peace the moment I stopped observing and allowed myself to be dragged into the drama. When life appeared to be happening to me, I was in a state of agitation. When I saw life as nothing more than things happening, and I stopped personalizing those things, I was at peace.

It no longer mattered all that much that I was in prison. Reality was what it was and I no longer sought to alter it. I was learning to accept things exactly as they were, and to work within reality as opposed to attempting to force my desires and expectations on reality. Soon I would find these realizations tested.

I met an inmate named Pete. Pete was a man with a very long prison sentence. His crime, however, was non-violent. This meant that he was able to progress to a low-security facility like the one we were in. But unlike prisoners such as myself, he was not going home any time soon. My sentence was not that long, therefore I would likely be accepted to a halfway house in the near future. This fact irritated men like Pete. He saw countless people progress into this prison only to be released a short time later, while he was forever left behind.

Pete was a small and timid man. This fact meant that he suffered from a complex. He knew himself to be weak, but wanted to be perceived as strong and hard. He had a habit of picking fights with men he knew were going to be released soon. Such men were not likely to want to fight him, so he would attempt to convince everyone that they chose not to fight because they feared him. This allowed him to create a false image of himself. The interesting thing was that everyone knew what he was doing. He was fooling no one but himself, and I doubt very much that he was successful even at that.

I ended up getting a maintenance job at the prison, which is where I met Pete. He and I were assigned to work together. He seemed friendly and helpful at first. He asked many questions about me and my sentence, and he quickly learned that I would likely be leaving soon. I didn't know it at the time, but this made me the next target of his little game.

My life had thus settled into a routine. I went to work in the mornings with the maintenance crew. Pete became increasingly irritating, but I mostly ignored him and focused on doing my job. In the afternoons, I worked out. Evenings were spent meditating and talking with other inmates. Before long, I even made another friend in prison, a man named Ben, with whom I got along very well. He and I spent much time talking and playing chess. Prison life had become something altogether different from what it had been, and I couldn't help wondering how much of this change was created by me.

• • •

"God-damned fucking bitch!" James shouted as he came into the cell one evening.

I looked up from the book I was reading. "What's the matter, James," I asked.

"That cunt is still tryin' to make my life miserable," he replied.

That seemed a strange thing for James to say. I wondered how she could be impacting his life at all. I laid my book down and observed him. I liked James. I knew that he had problems, but he was still a very likable guy. He was friendly and considerate—a bit self-obsessed, maybe, but then, aren't we all?

"What happened, James?" I asked.

"My case manager gave me a write-up," he answered.

You get a write up when you break the prison rules. What this had to do with his ex-girlfriend was beyond me.

"What did he write you up for?" I asked.

James paced about the cell. He was angry, agitated.

"Improper use of the phones," he answered.

I stared at him a moment. "What did you do, James?"

"Nuthin," he snapped.

"James…"

"That bitch called my case manager and told him I tried to call her," he said.

The prison phone system is different from phones in the real world. If you have friends or family who will send you money, that money is kept in an account that you can use for canteen items or phone calls. You have to submit a list of people you would like to call along with their phone numbers. If they are approved, you can then call them. You enter your personal code into the phone along with a two-digit speed dial code for the person you want to call. This makes it basically impossible to call anyone who is not approved.

"How do they say you managed to do that?" I asked.

"That's just it," he said. "I didn't call her. I can't call her."

"Let me see the write up," I said.

James handed me the yellow slip of paper.

"It says here that you had a friend call her and give her a message from you, James," I said.

"Yeah, my friend called her. I didn't"

"Doesn't she have a restraining order against you?" I asked.

"So?"

"James, you know that a restraining order means that you cannot contact her in any way. That means you can't have a friend send her messages. You could get new criminal charges for that."

"I hate that bitch," he said. "She's out to get me."

This was typical of James. To him, this was not something he had done; it was instead something that was being done to him. James was in love with this woman, but it was a sick, twisted love that wasn't really love at all. He felt as if he possessed her, as if she was his to do with as he wanted, therefore any attempt to stop him was unfair.

"What did you expect, James?" I asked. "Do you think that if you can talk to her all will be well between you two?"

"I can't believe she's out to get me like this," he said. "I've been nothing but good to her, and this is the thanks I get."

I sat stunned over these words. *How could he say such a thing?* "You've been nothing but good to her?" I asked. "What the hell are you talking about?"

James looked at me quizzically.

"James," I continued, my voice betraying my irritation. "I've been listening to you talk about her for a while now. You acted as if you owned her, as if she was yours to do with as you willed. You still act as if she exists only to please you. When she wanted out from under your dominance, you were mean to her, rude to her. She finally left you, and what did you do? You stalked her and terrorized her, then finally you beat the shit out of her. You beat her so badly, they sent you to prison over it, and now you continue to torment her from in here by having a friend send her messages. You have the audacity to sit there and tell me you were nothing but good to her?"

A look of horror came over James, followed quickly by a look of pure hatred. "Fuck you!" he shouted as he leapt to his feet and hovered over me. His fists were clenched and I thought he might attack me. "Who the fuck do you think you are talking to me like that!" He made a jerking motion toward me with his right fist as if he wanted to hit me. I stood slowly, staring into his eyes with a look meant to convey to him that it would be a big mistake to attack me. "Just who the fuck do you think you are talking to me like that?" he asked.

I said nothing. I simply stared, my senses on full alert, prepared to do whatever I might have to do.

"Fuck you!" he shouted and he stormed out of the cell.

I sat down on my bunk and attempted to calm myself. That was a close call. I learned something very important that day. This new-found insight of mine was a wonderful tool, but it could also be a terrible weapon. It was wrong of me to do what I did to James. In that moment, I sought to fix him when he would have been better served had I instead been a friend to him and just listened. People often need their denials. It is their coping mechanism. To deprive them of that is an act of cruelty. I wanted to convince myself that I was acting in James' best interest, that I was telling him what he needed to hear, but I was not. The truth was that I had grown irritated with his denial and sought to rub it in his face. My motives were not born of kindness. They were instead an act of violence against him born of my dislike for what he was doing. This was something Ray would never have done to me.

I realized that day that there was a huge burden of responsibility I had to assume. It was important that I become very aware of my motives and that I act only out of kindness, never out of spite. I should have listened to James, been a friend to him, and offer small bits of advice that would help him come to this realization on his own. I instead took it upon myself to force this realization upon him. I determined then and there that I would never do such a thing again.

James returned to the cell at lockdown. He was a beaten and dejected man. My brilliant insight had done nothing but inflict unnecessary pain.

"I owe you an apology, James," I said. "I had no business talking to you like that."

"It's okay," James replied. "I'm over it."

He wasn't, but I knew better than to push the matter further. I rolled over and went to sleep.

CHAPTER FIFTEEN

Everything we hear is an opinion, not a fact. Everything we see is a perspective, not the truth. – Marcus Aurelius

Pete continued his provocations. I continued to ignore them. The more I ignored them, the bolder he became. Soon he was bossing me around and making snide remarks regarding my work. I'd like to say that my new-found spiritual realization exalted me to such heights that I could rise above such things. I'd like to say that I was now a saint—I wasn't. I've learned that spiritual awareness is not a goal you seek to attain. It is, instead, a path that you set yourself on. Life still did the things life always did, and me, being human, sometimes handled things well, and other times handled things not so well. One day, after completing a repair on one of the air conditioning units, Pete came up and laid into me.

"What the fuck kind of work is this?" he asked caustically.

I rolled my eyes thinking, "Here he goes again." I ignored him

"I can't believe you're that fucking stupid," he said.

My anger surged inside of me. I could break this little runt of a man with one hand and I knew it. The other inmates were watching to see how I would react. I took a deep breath and spoke calmly. "I did what I was instructed to do, Pete," I said.

"Oh," he said sarcastically. "And I suppose you were told to do the shoddiest repair work possible?" he asked.

And that was it. Life had drawn me in. I was no longer formulating an appropriate response, I was now reacting. I was at the mercy of my emotions, and the overwhelming emotion I felt was anger.

My eyes narrowed and went cold. "Back the fuck off, Pete," I said sternly.

Pete had the upper hand here. There were two possible outcomes now that I had opened my mouth, and he knew it. The first option, I would back down. The second, I would attack Pete and beat the shit out of him. He didn't care which. If I backed down, he could act like a badass and tell everyone I was afraid of him. If I beat the shit out of him, I would be regressed and he would win the satisfaction of knowing he prevented me from going home. My reaction played right into his game.

"You think you're bad?" he said. "Let's handle this right fucking now."

I stood staring at him. I knew full well my dilemma. This is what happens when you react as opposed to taking the time to respond. My anger was raging and it wanted me to react further by beating the shit out of this man. I came very, very close to giving in to that anger. It would have felt good to hit him, but it would not have felt so good two minutes later. I learned that day that I still had a choice. I did not have to let my emotions win. Standing there on the brink of disaster, I could still open up a space in which to formulate a response, and that was what I did. "I'll tell you what, Pete," I said. The guards are right around the corner, so I don't want to handle this right now. Come to my cell later and we will take care of it there." This was a perfect response. Pete was in a different unit from me and prisoners were not allowed to be in any unit other than their own. If he came to my cell to fight, chances were we would not get caught. But if we did, he would be in my unit and in my cell, making him appear the aggressor. I could claim self-defense and avoid getting into trouble. I then turned and walked away.

My friend Ben was in a cell across the hall from me. I went to him after work that day.

"Keep an eye out for Pete," I said. "If you see him coming toward my cell, let me know."

"What happened?" Ben asked.

"He seems to think he wants to fight me," I said.

"Pete does? You'll break him in two."

"I doubt he'll show up," I replied. "But keep an eye out just the same."

"Will do, my brother," Ben replied. Then he added, "I hope he does come so I can watch you smash him."

I smiled. By now my anger had subsided and I was not so keen on doing violence to Pete. But I was prepared to do whatever needed to be done. I went into my cell to meditate.

Ben was beside himself and thought to offer me some advice. "What you do," he said, "is stand here holding the door to your cell. As he comes in, slam it into his head. That'll teach him."

I thanked Ben for his advice, and he returned to his cell across the hall. Pete never showed up. He spent the next few days trying to convince everyone that I was afraid to fight him. But the word on the yard was that I invited him to my cell to fight and he never showed. Pete told everyone he could his version of events, while I said nothing to anyone. Try as he might, Pete could not convince people that his version was true. He was trying to force reality into being something it wasn't. There was no need for me to say anything because reality was what it was. It didn't need me as its advocate. Pete never bothered me again, and a few days later, he was transferred to another job. He became a non-issue.

I soon became aware of more changes that were taking place in me. The first indication this was happening did not come from anything in me at all. It came from those around me. I began to notice that people were coming to me to talk about whatever problems were on their minds. People were seeking me out for council and advice. This had never happened to me before. I often wanted to give advice, but people never wanted to hear it. Now they sought it from me. It reminded me of Ray and the way people sought him. I knew that I was becoming something I had never been before.

I met a young kid named Josh. He went by the nickname Skittles. Don't ask me why he would choose such a nickname. It was a stupid name, and it was fitting because Josh was such a stupid kid. He was incredibly irritating, but he was likable just the same. He came into my cell one evening to visit. We spent some time talking, then the subject turned to more serious matters. I had begun journaling by this time, and I wrote the following entry.

> *I helped a young man today. His name is Josh (Skittles). He is 25 years old, and he has spent his entire adult life in prison. I asked him about his parents. He never knew his father. His mother passed away when he was 15 years old. She died a slow death from diabetes. His aunt and uncle took him in but he soon ran away. He said he was running from dealing with his Mom's death. I asked if he had grieved her since. He said, "No."*
>
> *I spoke with him further, and he said he felt bad because he did not do enough to help his dying mother. He also said he was mean to her. I told him he faced a true dilemma: he could not truly grieve his mother's death without first forgiving himself. I then told him his mother already forgave him. She knew that her 15 year old son was struggling with her illness and impending death, and that he could not cope. She even knew that his angry*

behavior toward her was a natural reaction—he was angry she was leaving him and he expressed it from time to time even though he felt guilty doing so. I told him she knew all of this and that she forgave him before she died.

I told him that her dying wish was that he would one day forgive himself. I saw him fight back the tears as I spoke. I lightened the mood so he would not embarrass himself. This kid who never listens to anyone actually heard me. It was a beautiful moment.

My life in prison was filled with many events such as this. I no longer focused on me and what I wanted. I shifted my focus onto others and what I could do for them. I became a healing influence in the lives of the people around me. People reacted to me positively; my life was enriched by the experience. The strangest thing of all was that this change was happening *in prison*. That's the last place you would ever expect such a thing to happen. But that is exactly where it was happening. Hardened convicts reacted to me in an entirely new way. My life was no longer about anger and violence; it was instead about helping those around me.

I was following my intuition more and more. I have no idea where the words came from that I spoke to this kid. After all, I don't really know what his mother thought. But at the time the words seemed to come to me out of nowhere. There was a time when I would not have uttered such things, thinking them foolish. Now it felt as if there was a voice greater than me that was speaking through me, and I let it speak rather than stand in its way. It was this voice that had a healing effect on people. I had stopped trying to live the godly life—that was just my ego trying to be all holy and altruistic. I instead began getting myself out of the way so that this thing we refer to as God could begin living my life.

I continued my meditation, and before I knew it, my thoughts slowed down. The time between thoughts became greater and greater. It was then that I learned a most remarkable thing. Each thought carried with it an emotion. The emotion seemed to follow the thought. So a thought would pop into my head, then the associated emotion would begin to rise. But before that emotion made it into conscious awareness, the next thought would pop into my head and the next emotion would begin to rise. This happened over and over all day so that I had all of these emotions rising up from within me, but none of them made it into consciousness. These emotions were causing a constant state of agitation in my body, but because I was unaware of them, I could do nothing about them. These emotions were making it difficult for me to meditate. The anxiety I felt in my body was caused by incessant emotions swimming around in the other than conscious part of my mind. I learned this as my thoughts began to slow. As they slowed, the space between the thoughts became greater. Soon the space was long enough that the emotion associated with the thought had time to come into consciousness. I became aware of the emotions that were caused by each and every thought.

I realized that the agitation caused by these unconscious emotions drove me to seek relief from the agitation through distractions. I would do anything to relieve this agitation. I would go play chess with Ben, read a book, work out, anything to distract me from the feelings hovering just beyond my awareness. I realized that this same agitation was what caused me to seek distraction through drug use. This was the source of the pain that caused me to seek relief through drugs. I had always looked for the cause for this behavior in events outside of me. I was now beginning to see that the root of the problem had been inside of me all along. It was the noise in my head that led to the emotional agitation. This agitation was the root cause of the pain that led to drug use. The drug use led to prison. It was my head, my very own thoughts, my thinking that resulted in my imprisonment. Ray's story about the South Indian monkey trap came to mind. I had finally looked within, and I found that the cause of my problem was me.

The more I meditated, the more I learned about my mind and the suffering my thinking had caused. I learned the difference between pain and suffering. Painful events happen. But pain is fleeting. It comes over you like a wave. It grows, crests and subsides very quickly. If I just let the pain do what it does, it is over very soon. But that was not what I had done. As pain grew in intensity, as it neared its crest, my thinking would then kick in. It would say things like, "This is so unfair. I don't deserve this. This should not be happening to me." This thinking became the energy feeding the pain so that the wave of pain would never subside. Thus my pain became suffering. A painful event that would have subsided in an hour or so now became an event over which I could suffer for twenty years. It was my thinking that turned pain into suffering. Pain happened to me. Suffering I did to myself.

My thoughts continued to slow, and as they did, I discovered ever more emotions that were being fueled by my thinking. I began to realize that I was expending untold amounts of energy on the thoughts that were feeding these emotions. I fueled my own suffering. I noticed that I no longer had to do this. All of this was happening outside of conscious awareness, and as I became aware of each new thought and its associated emotion, I was able to let each emotional state go. One by one, all of these hitherto hidden emotions fell away. I felt not only relief from these emotional states, I felt the return of the energy that had been spent maintaining them. I felt more alive, less tired and drained all of the time. I had been wearing myself out, feeding negative emotional states with the energy of constant thinking. I was doing all of this without the slightest awareness that any of it was happening. No wonder I felt myself to be a victim of life.

Until now, there had been no way to put an end to any of this because I was utterly unaware that any of it was happening. The only way to become aware of it, I found, was through meditation.

I was finding my purpose. And it was this thought that led to a question for which I found no easy answer. I had learned that the attempt to serve my needs, wants and desires led to nothing but suffering. Giving of myself to others led to a sense of peace and belonging. This meant that my purpose was to give to others, but the question that I could not answer was, where did this purpose come from? I could not escape the feeling that this purpose was decided for me by something other than me. This led to a confrontation with the idea known as God.

Peace came to me with the realization that I was a part of something larger than me. But I was resistant to the idea of God as I had been taught. The concept of an anthropomorphic being sitting in a place called heaven, judging everything I do, seemed so small and trivial. And it also seemed to be very egocentric. I mean, after all, would an omniscient, omnipotent being really take a personal interest in everything I was doing? That seemed like my ego running out of control. This does not mean to imply that I am not important. Clearly I was beginning to play an important, and even necessary, role in people's lives, but I thought it mistaken to think that this was in any way *about* me. It was better for me to not see myself in such grandiose terms.

What I came to was the realization that life has a wisdom all its own. Resist that wisdom, and I suffer. Surrender to it, and I am at peace. I cannot say *why* this works. I cannot say *how* it works. I can only say that I have found it *to* work. The fact that it does work is enough. So I began to believe in this fact itself as God. God was no longer a man; he was instead a process for living that led to peace. There was no need to understand or explain; it couldn't be understood or explained anyway. This did not alter the fact that it was effective. So I abandoned the idea of proving the existence of

God as nothing more than another distraction. And as I did so, my meditations began to reveal things I never dreamed possible.

I am reluctant now to even use the word God because it carries with it so much baggage that really does not apply. Yet I have no other word to use. For that reason, I want to make it as clear as I can what I mean when I use the word. When I speak of God, I am speaking of something like an intelligent, animating energy. I am speaking of the wisdom of life. I am speaking of the path to peaceful existence, acceptance and joy. It is not an entity; it is instead an expression. Everything, and everyone is a part of that expression. I am but a temporary manifestation of that universal expression people have historically referred to as God. All people are that manifestation, and in that lies their true expression, their beauty, their power and meaning.

I cannot describe it more clearly, and at best this description is a fuzzy indication of what I mean. Words are funny things born of the finite mind. They are completely incapable of encapsulating the infinite. They can, at best approximate it, point toward it, but never fully describe it. The concept of God is something that can only be experienced, never described. It would be like attempting to describe the flavor of a peach to someone who had never tasted one. I can speak of sweet and I can speak of juicy. But to truly know the flavor, you must taste it for yourself.

Now that my mind had, at long last, grown quiet, meditation began to rocket me into realizations of the most profound nature. My eyes opened, and I could see the reality that had always existed before me. After each meditation session, I wrote in my journal of the realizations that came to me. I could attempt to describe these to you, but my journal entries during this time say it best.

Meditation beginning to bring real benefits. Beginning to see things more clearly. Saw today that Lucifer, Mara, the devil— whatever you want to call it—is in reality me—or my ego. It promises me satisfaction, yet never satisfies. My thinking, my thoughts, are links in chains that bind me to this existence, to my suffering. They dissolve when the light of focused concentration reveals their true nature. They have no true nature. They are empty, hollow, as I am empty, hollow. Everything seems to be nothing. I seem to be nothing but a tension in the universe. I cannot explain it; I can only experience it. My words can, at best, only point toward it. The story of Lucifer's pride, thinking he was greater than God, his separation from God and casting out of heaven, is all metaphor. That story is a mythological representation of the human separation from God. I am trapped in a prison of my own making. I bind myself with thoughts. All thoughts lead to suffering. The ego is like a slimy fish you cannot keep hold of. It keeps wriggling and slipping away. I am just beginning to subdue it. I see now how skewed my vision is. I cannot see the world as it is; I see it through my crazy thinking and associations that totally alter what I think I see. At least I see that now. I must dissolve all preconceptions and soon I will see the world as it is.

When I say that these realizations came to me, I must be very clear that it was not something my thinking mind figured out. It was actually the opposite. My thinking mind grew quiet, and this made it possible for me to hear the voice of the universe in the form of intuition. These ideas were not puzzles that I had solved. They were what was left when I stopped trying to solve puzzles. I wrote them in the language available to me. I don't really believe in Lucifer. That word is just a symbol to describe our self-created mental dramas that manifest as if our emotions are foreign bodies possessing us. I find it more practical to think of Bible stories as metaphor.

The old stories speak of demon possession as a foreign body that takes over. Is that not an apt description of emotion? Are we not slaves to our emotions? I find that my life had been one in which I believed whatever my emotions were telling me. I was now beginning to find a means through which I could break my bondage to my emotional states. I was beginning to see that emotional states were driven by memories of past events. It was this perception that drove me. My emotions surged, then I acted as one possessed by something other than me. How many times did I act in such a situation, only to regret it later? How many times did I get angry and immediately fire off that email, send that text message, or say those words that, the following morning, I wished I could take back. I was now able to delay such reactions.

It is interesting that I have never regretted waiting before engaging in some action or another. I have many times regretted not waiting, however. I can see how this would be called demon possession. It is as if something takes over, commits me to a course of action, then disappears, leaving me with the consequences. When I later find myself back in my "right mind," I wonder how it was that I behaved so foolishly. I was beginning to free myself from this behavior by observing it. This took from me the urgent need to act. The emotion would subside, then I could respond rather than react. I could say that God saved me from the demons that possessed me. But what this really means is that I am no longer a slave to the emotional states that once drove me. Words are but symbols used to describe the world around us. It makes me no difference which symbols a person chooses to use.

I thought of Ray often. So many of the things he had told me before, things that made no sense to me, suddenly became crystal clear. My eyes were at last opening to that which Ray had long ago begun to see. I missed Ray and I wanted to share these new experiences with him. Unfortunately that was not possible. The prison system does not allow convicts to write to other convicts.

Charles Bynum

CHAPTER SIXTEEN

In the sky, there is no distinction of east and west;
people create distinctions out of their own minds and then believe them
to be true. – The Buddha

"Why do you sit there and do that shit all the time?" James asked one evening before lights out.

"Do what shit?" I asked.

"Meditate like that," he answered. "Every time I come in here you're sitting there staring off into space."

"I find it helps me."

"How can sitting there doing nothing help you?" he asked.

James was not interested in learning about meditation. I sensed that he had something else on his mind that he wanted to talk about, and this was his way of leading into the conversation. I decided to follow along.

"I've found that when my mind gets quiet, I begin to see things that I couldn't see before," I said.

"Seems stupid to me."

"Probably is stupid," I replied. "But what else is there for me to do in here?"

"My mind races all the time, it's always thinking something," James said.

"Everyone's mind does that. Meditation can change that, but it's a difficult thing to do."

"I tried it once, didn't do anything for me."

"I hear that all the time," I replied. "People try it once or twice then give up. It takes a strong commitment and a lot of practice before you see any benefits. It's like wanting to learn to play the piano. You sit down once or twice, find you cannot play, so you quit. You'll never learn that way. The people who are good at playing the piano spend many hours practicing."

"So you are practicing meditation?" he asked.

"Yeah," I answered. "It's mostly practice. I spend very little time in what could actually be called true meditation. I'm not that good at it yet."

"What happens when you are truly meditating?"

I smiled. "It is the most remarkable thing," I answered. "There are times when my mind slows down, the thoughts stop racing, and suddenly, I find myself completely immersed in the moment. Actually that's not quite right. I find myself immersed in the here and now."

James cocked his head to the side. "What's the difference between the moment and the here and now?" he asked.

I smiled. "Good question," I replied. "This is itself one of the things that comes to you when your mind grows still. I began to see what these things we call moments really are. We experience everything in these small increments of time that we call moments. But we never ask what a moment is. But think about this, James. Look at this book here." I picked up a book that was lying next to me on my bunk. "In order for you to see this book, light has to be reflected off it. That light is detected by your eyes, then that light is converted into an electrical signal that travels down the optical nerve to your brain. Once it hits the brain, your mind interacts with it. Your mind determines its shape and its color, categorizes it as a book, and only then do you become aware of it. This all happens very fast, but, by the time you are aware of the moment, it is already in the past. Not only that, you have described it to yourself. This means that you have not experienced the book directly, you have instead perceived it. And that perception carries with it all kinds of assumptions based upon your personal memories. The act of seeing the book is kind of like a black and white picture that your mind receives. The thoughts that you apply to it are like the crayons you use to color the picture. What ends up in your mind is a combination of that which you perceived, colored by that which you remember. I think that is why moments seem like such small segments of time. Your mind requires that small slice of time to describe to itself what it is seeing. This means that we see life as a continual stream of moments, one after another. When you quiet the mind, you begin to simply experience what is, without your mind coloring it. That is the here and now, experience without the mind's intervention. The here and now is eternal. It is what has always been and what will forever be. It is a very moving experience."

James stared at me blankly.

"Sorry," I said. "I know it sounds a bit crazy."

"What's the point in all of that?" he asked.

"Well, for me, two things have begun to happen. First, I've been able to see how much of what I think reality to be is really nothing but my own personal thoughts imposed upon reality. A book is a very simple example, but if I look at something more complex, say a woman, what is my mind then doing to that image?"

"What do you mean?" James asked.

"When I see a woman, all kinds of mental thoughts begin to color my image of her. I have memories of my relationship with my mother. I often have sexual thoughts and feelings. I have memories of past relationships, such as the painful memories of my marriage. All of these things begin to color my experience of any new woman I meet. Before I know it, I'm not seeing this new woman at all. I am instead reacting to memories that now have her face on them. This colors my reality and often prevents me from seeing things as they are."

"How does that stop you from seeing things as they are?" he asked.

"Well…" I said as I paused to consider my next words. "Let's say I meet a woman who acts in ways that unconsciously reminds me of my mother. I would then begin to color my image of this woman with my past experiences of my mother. I might think her to be kind and generous and loving and all of those things I associate with my mom. She might, in reality, be the most evil, lying manipulative person to ever walk the planet. But I won't be able to see that. I am seeing my memories of mom projected onto her. She could then cause me all kinds of harm, and I would be defenseless to stop it. I might even think I've fallen in love with her because she reminds me of all those things I loved about Mom. But what I'm really falling in love with is my own mental image, not her. Inevitably, she proceeds to act according to her true nature, and I get angry. She is not acting according to my projection, how dare her! Then I seek to change or alter her behavior to suit my fantasy that I carry in my head, and all kinds of strife will ensue. She is probably projecting her images onto me at the same time, and this causes even more difficulty. Neither of us really loves the other, because neither of us can really see the other. We are in love with our projected fantasies and we end up hating one another for being something other than what we wanted each other to be."

James sat silently. He was thinking of his girlfriend.

"It can happen the other way around too," I added.

"What do you mean?" he asked.

"The woman may be honest, compassionate and kind. But she may exhibit a behavior that reminds me of my ex-wife. Now I project upon her all kinds of fears related to what I experienced in my marriage. Soon I am accusing her of motives she may not possess. I see her as dangerous when in fact she is not. The truth is, we actually do a combination of these things. Sometimes we project our fantasies, other times we project our fears. Either way, we are actually reacting to memories, not the person standing before us."

"What good does all of this do you?" he asked.

"It changes how I approach reality," I answered. "Think about this a moment. Let's say that, instead of projecting memories onto her, I simply observe her as she is. I observe myself also—this is very important. I must observe her *and* me. Observing me, I begin to see my feelings that I think are love, but because I am observing as opposed to reacting, I see them as remnants of memories of my mother—they have nothing to do with this woman. Because I can now see this, I choose to let those feeling pass and not be guided by them. Let's say I then I see her behaving dishonestly. Since I am not attempting to project my fantasies upon her, I can see her dishonesty as something inherent in her. I no longer feel the need to coerce her into being something other than who she is. I can now see that this is just her. I have no need to change her or turn her into what I want her to be. I can see that she is perhaps not the right person for me and I can simply remove myself from the situation. Or, I observe myself and see my memories of my ex-wife coming to the surface. I let these feelings pass and stop projecting them on the woman standing before me. I can now see her as she is, and the wonderful experience of her true being is available to me where it would not have been before. Either outcome is positive."

"You learned all this from meditation?' he asked.

"I did," I replied. "I didn't just learn it, I began to observe it. It's one thing to be told this; it is quite another to actually see it.

Meditation afforded me the opportunity to see it happening, and that gave me the ability to begin to change it.

"Do you think this is what I've been doing with my girlfriend?" he asked.

"Only you can determine that," I answered. "But if you think about it, it is possible that you projected your fantasies upon her, began to see that she was not who you thought her to be, then in desperation, attempted to force her to conform to the image in your mind. When we do things like that, we feel like it is the other person's fault we are behaving badly. 'If she would just act right, I wouldn't behave this way,' is what we are tempted to think. The truth is, she is acting in accordance with who she is. My inability to accept that is what is really driving my behavior."

"I never thought about it that way before," he said.

"And I cannot tell you that this is what is really going on. You have to come to that yourself."

It would not have surprised me to learn that James found it difficult to fall asleep that night, much like those nights I had spent with Ray. It was interesting that the mistake that I had made with James earlier by confronting him with ideas he was not ready to accept, now seemed to be working toward the greater good. My words hurt James, but they also seemed to soften him up, to make him open to what I was saying now. Life seems to act that way. Life is incredibly efficient—it uses both our strengths and our weaknesses to further its designs. Even our mistakes are put to use in the service of the greater good, though we often do not see this. This realization helped to free me from my desire to be "perfect." I need only be what I am, and I need only to trust that life will do with me what needs to be done. There is real freedom in that.

CHAPTER SEVENTEEN

Thinking begins only when we have come to know that reason, glorified for centuries, is the stiff-necked adversary of thought. – Martin Heidegger

I wish I could say that these new-found realizations made life so much easier for me. Actually, I could say this, and in a sense it would be true. But the fact is that staying mindful of my emotional states was a very difficult endeavor. Life, it seems, tempts one into emotional entanglements. Every emotion that pops into my head is yet another instance of life luring me into suffering. My daily challenge was to be ever more aware of the times when this was happening. I struggled with this often, worked hard on recognizing that it was happening, and strove to return to a state of peaceful acceptance every time I found myself drawn into the drama. I wrote of this in my journal after my meditation sessions.

Everything—absolutely everything tempts me into my ego and out of my true nature. My true being is an essence, not an entity. As an entity, I am apart from all else, as an essence, I am a part of. The men here push ego in various competitive ways. This is an utterly useless attempt to compensate for a lack of oneness with the all by asserting the very cause of the problem with force. Ego separates me from God. I experience the void as insecurity. I assert ego even harder in an attempt to relieve the insecurity. My separation with God thus grows, the void deepens. I am attempting to solve the problem by applying more of the cause of the problem. This is what the Tao te Ching means when it says, "The path into the light appears dark." We believe ego to be the cure for insecurity when it is in fact the cause. Destroying the ego would seem to leave us utterly helpless, yet that is the path back. I am tempted into competition each day. To compete and win leads to separation from God. To compete and lose also leads to separation from God. I create all of these ego temptations then I fall for them. There are so many. How can I ever overcome them all?

Ego is meant to be a tool through which the God essence interacts in the material world. Unfortunately we begin to identify with the tool (ego) and thereby lose touch with our God essence. The key is learning to use the tool yet not identify with it. "Be in this world but not of it," is another way of saying the same thing.

I already know how to worship something with all my heart, all my mind, and all my soul. I have, thus far, worshiped my ego as such. Though I would never admit it in words, I have through my actions proven my belief that my ego was God. I then identified with that ego turning me into God. My every waking moment was thus spent in the service of My wants, My needs, My will, My desire. This me, this ego I served, is not real. It is empty. It is not even alive; it is dead. My struggle now is to serve the God image that is in me. Abandon my will—my ego nature—and serve that other that is in me. The more I do that, the more alive I become. Ego has a million tricks to keep itself alive. Even my altruistic acts of following the will of God get usurped and used to reinforce the ego. I must remain ever vigilant and watch my mind as it attempts to weave ego into everything. I must dissolve me into God. I must return to the one from whence I came. This is my struggle. Some days I do better than others.

Each day it became more and more clear that it was my own mind, my own thinking that caused all of my troubles. Life continued to do the things it always did, but I now had a choice regarding my response to life. I also recognized that it was unreasonable to expect that I could do this perfectly in every situation. I am, after all, a human being, and this meant that I would do better sometimes than others. It was all exactly as it should be, and life did not need me meddling in affairs trying to make them conform to my idea of "better." I would soon learn that the things I thought of as positive could cause me just as much strife as the things I thought of as negative.

I was sitting alone in my cell one day shortly after lunch when I heard my name called on the intercom instructing me to report to my case-manager's office. I got off my bunk, walked out of the unit and headed to the building where the case manager's offices were located.

"Come in," my case manager said smiling. "How are you today?" he asked.

"I'm doing well," I answered, suspicious of what he wanted. A call to the case manager's office was often the result of some infraction you were being accused of committing. I was wracking my brain trying to figure out what I could have possibly done that would have resulted in a reprimand, or worse, a write-up.

"I have some good news for you," he said.

I looked at him suspiciously. "Really," I replied. "What?"

"I put your name in for Community Corrections, and you've been accepted."

I sat stunned. Community Corrections was a halfway house program that allowed offenders who were doing well to begin their transition back into the real world. Being accepted meant that I would be living in a facility in my home town, where I could get a job and begin to interact in a non-prison environment. There are no fences or guards; you leave the facility each day and return to sleep at night. It also meant that my chances of being paroled early were greatly enhanced. I was speechless.

"Congratulations," the case manager continued. "As soon as a bed comes available, you will be leaving prison."

My head was spinning. "How long will that be?" was all I could think to say.

"The wait can be anywhere up to six months," he answered. "But the average wait has been running about ninety days."

I wish I could describe to you what I was feeling. A light suddenly appeared at the end of a long, dark tunnel. The nightmare of prison was coming to an end. There are no words with which I can describe what this feels like—they simply do not exist.

"Thank you," I said, and despite my best effort, tears flowed from my eyes. I quickly wiped them away.

"I have some papers here for you to sign," he continued. "I've enrolled you in the re-entry class the prison offers for those who are leaving. You'll begin attending those classes on Monday."

"Is there anything else I need to do?" I asked.

"No, just wait till we call you to let you know you're leaving. You won't be notified until the night before you go."

I thanked him again and returned to my cell. Ben came to see me.

"Well?" he asked.

"I've been accepted to ComCor," I answered.

"Alright!" he exclaimed. "Charles is getting out of here."

"Yeah, can you believe that?" I asked.

"If anyone deserves to get out of this place, you do, my brother," he said. Then he left my cell and began telling anyone who would listen that I was going home.

That was, by any definition, the best news anyone could have given me. You would think that I would have been so happy that I would be beside myself. But this wasn't the case at all. It was two months before a bed was available, and I swear those were the worst two months of my life.

Prison became absolutely unbearable. Knowing I would be leaving soon caused me to hate where I was. All the newfound peace and acceptance I had found went right out the door. I wanted out, and my obsession over getting out made the here and now miserable for me. Meditation became increasingly difficult because it was nearly impossible to quiet a mind obsessed with leaving prison. The other inmates irritated the hell out of me because all I could think of was how great it would be to be able to interact with normal people again. I was living in an imaginary world of what my life would soon be, and this made the world of what my life was miserable. During my time in prison, I had taught myself how to deal with painful and difficult circumstance with acceptance and serenity. Now I was having to learn how to apply that same serenity and acceptance to positive events.

This is when it really came clear to me how important it is to *always* accept life just exactly as it is. Any projection, positive or negative, takes one out of the here and now, and places us in a position of wanting life to somehow be other than what it is. This is the true cause of suffering. My reality was that I was still in prison. I then compared that reality to a mental construct of what I wanted my life to be. Since what my life was fell short of what I hoped my life would someday soon be, I was unhappy. I took the best news I could ever have hoped to receive, and used it to make myself suffer.

Eager anticipation became the bane of my existence. I continued my meditation practice, but more often than not, I ended up feeling nothing but increased anxiety as my mind continued to wander in the fantasy of the life that awaited me. I practiced accepting even this anticipation, and I worked hard at allowing it to be what it was and I tried breathing through it. The times when I was successful at this led to some of the most productive meditation sessions I had ever experienced. I wrote about the realizations that were now coming to me during those times.

> *I experienced my first ever true glimpse of emptiness yesterday. It only lasted a moment, then I tried to label the experience with words. As the words came into my head, the experience left me. I wish I would have just let the experience be instead of trying to describe it to myself with words. Who was I describing it to? I want to wrap everything in reason...silly me.*

> *I've found that the here and now is everything. The here and now is the cure for all suffering. If my mind wanders into the past or the future, I lose God. I return to the here and now and find him again.*

I finally began to realize that the here and now was everything at the very time when I absolutely despised being trapped in the here and now. I wanted to live in the there and then, but I was stuck. The there and then was not real, the here and now was. I desired that which was not real over that which was real. Fluctuating between acceptance of where I was, and the overwhelming desire to be elsewhere, became the most difficult spiritual practice of my life. I would never have thought of such a thing as being spiritual practice. I tend to think of spiritual practice as something much more sublime, like contemplating the essence of God, or some silly such thing. But spiritual practice is not like that at all. Spiritual practice is whatever you have to do to accept things as they are. For me, this meant letting go of my desire to leave, and accepting instead life as it was, right then, right there, in prison. And I hated it. My next journal entry said it all.

> *Ego won another round and I became utterly distracted, irritated, annoyed, in a word—suffering. My desire to leave prison drove me into ego. Ego wants out, I cannot get out, I suffer. Ego always equates to suffering. I must meditate more. Having to share a cell makes this difficult, but not impossible. I must keep going. I feel my separation more than ever now. The two in me must be made one. I lost my mindfulness, I must now get it back.*

Charles Bynum

CHAPTER EIGHTEEN

The most beautiful people we have known are those who have known defeat, known suffering, known struggle, known loss, and have found their way out of the depths. These persons have an appreciation, a sensitivity, and an understanding of life that fills them with compassion, gentleness, and a deep loving concern. Beautiful people do not just happen. – Elizabeth Kubler Ross

"What the fuck's been bothering you?" Ben asked one evening. "You should be happy as hell, man. I mean, you're going home. But you walk around here looking like you got slapped away from the dinner table for farting. I don't get that." Ben always had a rather poetic command of the English language.

"Yeah, it's kinda stupid, isn't it?" I replied smiling.

"*Kinda* stupid?" Ben replied sarcastically. "Brother, you're way beyond *kinda* stupid. If they had a scale for this kind of thing, you'd be in the completely fucking retarded range."

"It's not quite as stupid as it seems," I replied.

"Oh really," Ben said. "You're going home soon and yet, you're miserable. Tell me how exactly that's not as stupid as it seems." Ben had a way of making me laugh at myself, and I often found it very therapeutic. This was no exception.

"I know," I said. "I'm an idiot. I really should be happy. The truth is I *am* happy."

"You don't look like any happy person I ever saw."

"Well…It's just that, ever since they told me I was going to be leaving soon, time seems to have slowed to a standstill. Minutes seem like days, and days seem like years. I mean, I was good till they told me I'd be getting out. But knowing I'm getting out makes every day I spend here nearly unbearable."

"It'll be over before you know it," Ben said. "Be happy dude. *You're going home!*"

He was right, and I knew it. I felt stupid. I was telling someone who would be in prison for God only knows how long how miserable I was over the fact that I had such a short time remaining. It seemed upside down, but it was what it was.

"I'm telling you, Ben," I continued. "It's miserable not knowing when they're going to call me to go home. Each day I wake up hoping today will be the day, and each day I'm disappointed. The guys working in laundry are sick of me by now."

When you are released from prison, you are given a state-issued set of street clothes. Or at least they call them street clothes. They're nothing I would ever choose to wear on the streets. The laundry department issues those clothes, so, the guys working in the laundry are the first non-staff people to know you're going home. Thus I checked with them every day to see if they had been instructed to get my street clothes ready yet.

"Man, just relax," Ben replied. "You're getting the fuck out of here. Just be happy it's coming to an end."

"Okay, Ben," I retorted. "Just wait till you're short-timing. I hope you remember these words when it's your time to get out. In fact, I hope you choke on them."

Ben laughed. "I got something *you* can choke on," he said.

"Get the hell out of here," I replied, and I could hear Ben laughing as he walked down the hallway.

So it was that two months ended up feeling like twenty years. It was a great opportunity to practice all that I had learned. I did say a great opportunity, not a welcome one. I hated every minute of it, but that sort of became a joke in itself. Try as I might, fight, kick, scream, whatever, I was stuck in prison until such time as I was not. I determined that I would make the best of it, use the time to practice this damned acceptance that seemed such a great idea before. It sucked now, but that's just the way life is sometimes. "Get over it," I often had to tell myself.

After about thirty days I was beginning to finally settle my mind down a bit, beginning to accept things as they were again, when the unthinkable happened. Ben came rushing into my cell one afternoon.

"Guess what man!" he said. "I got accepted to ComCor today."

"Great!" I exclaimed. "That means we'll be there together."

"Well, not exactly," he said. "There's two ComCor facilities in town. My case manager told me I'm not going to the same one you're going to."

"Oh, well that's too bad. But it's great that you're getting out too."

"It gets even better," Ben said.

"What do you mean, it gets better?"

"The one I'm going to has only has a two-week wait!" Ben's eyes were twinkling, betraying the fact that he was loving this. I could tell his presentation was well rehearsed. He knew how miserable the wait had been for me, now he had the opportunity to make it even more so.

Let me tell you something about Ben. Ben and I had become close friends, and we remain close to this day. So it wasn't that he was being mean. It was just too good an opportunity to poke fun at me. He had to do it. The truth is, I would have done the same to him had the situation been reversed.

"You're full of shit," I replied.

"No, dude," he said. "My case manager said the average wait right now is two weeks."

"So, you're leaving before me?" I asked.

"I am. Aren't you happy for me?"

If by "happy" he meant I wanted to strangle him at that moment, he would be right. "God damn," I said. "You're leaving before me." I still couldn't get my mind around it. And to make matters worse, the more miserable it made me, the happier it made him.

"I don't believe this," I said.

"Oh, come on man," he replied while nudging me with his elbow. "Tell me you're happy for me."

"You're loving this, aren't you?" I said.

"Every minute of it, my brother," he replied.

"Okay," I said. "I *am* happy for you. But you have to understand, I hate you right now also."

Ben's grin extended fully from one side of his face to the other. He was quite pleased with himself. "I knew you would," he said and he ran out of the cell shouting down the hallway, "I'm goin' home before Charles." It was so wonderful that he could have this moment at my expense. I didn't get much meditation done *that* evening.

And so began my final thirty days in prison. Each time I ran into Ben, I was met with the obligatory, "I'm goin home before you." I ignored him. And I loved him. And I hated him. You know how it is between close friends. As it turned out, the tables soon turned. After two weeks, I kept saying to him, "You're still here? I thought you were supposed to be gone by now." His two weeks turned into six, so I ended up leaving before him. There really is a God after all.

I continued my meditation as best I could. I also attended the transition classes, with Ben, in preparation for our departures. It was then that I had the most amazing revelation of all. While meditating, I began to see something that seemed at first absolutely insane. My mind resisted it, wanted to tell me that I was crazy, but I let it come into consciousness anyway. I had learned that the most profound insights are those we are most resistant to. So I abandoned my resistance. I wrote about it in my journal.

> *Could it be that I have lost myself? Perhaps in my utter isolation and loneliness I retreated into an illness I experience as life. I am now desperately trying to make myself well by sending messages, lessons, so I might realize I am sick and begin to heal. Could my ego be the manifestation of the illness of God? Have I constructed this entire universe as a distraction from loneliness? If God is sick, how might He heal? What is the solution to His loneliness? Did God desire something other than what is? Is all existence and all life God's struggle to be other than what he is? Is the solution for God to just be and stop toying with this fantasy he calls creation; this ego he calls me? Am I the illness? Am I the foreign body infecting the mind of God? I think, perhaps, I am. I am the disease. I am the pain. I am the suffering. More importantly, I am the distraction. I have no reality outside the mind of God. I am the delusion of God. It is not me struggling to awaken; it is God longing to awaken. God wishes to experience himself, but he has fallen into the trap of ego. If God has deprived himself of himself, imagine his joy when he is reunited. The other than God element in me must die, for there is no other than God in me. It is not that I am God; it is just that God is—I never was.*

I wanted to think of this as insane, yet something deep inside of me knew otherwise. This was a very frightening time. After all, I had now convinced myself that I was the insane delusion of a sick and twisted God. I decided not to try to make sense of it. I determined instead to just let it be. I remember Ray telling me that heaven is on the other side of hell. So if you find yourself in the middle of hell, take heart—you're halfway there. Somehow those words comforted me now. And by allowing them to simply be, I found my way to the next revelation.

Ok, now it seems that God must go too. It is no ego—no God. The two depend one upon the other. If one goes, the other goes with it. I must go beyond ego, beyond God. Then…nothing more can be said, and everything said says nothing.

There is a stillness in the center of all this motion. Find it.

And there it was. I had, at long last, broken through. I finally saw why the ancients refused to even assign God a name. Doing so reduced the infinite into something finite, something we mere mortals could understand. God is not something that human beings can ever understand. To even refer to him as God is to limit him. To call him God, is to collapse him into something finite, and it is this very act that ends up reinforcing the ego. To move beyond ego, and beyond God, is to move beyond mind. I am reminded of the Tao te Ching, when it said, "You cannot know it. You can only be it." I had realized a first-hand experience of the infinite that no words could ever describe because no mind could ever understand. The world had transformed into something utterly different than anything it had ever been before. But then, the world didn't really change at all. Nothing had changed; everything was as it had always been. Only now, I was able to see it as it was. I no longer struggled to force the world into what I wanted it to be. I resisted the temptation to abandon the here and now by moving into memories of the past, or projections of the future.

Another funny thing happened. The very next day after that last journal entry, I was released from prison. I was released to ComCor and was paroled a few months after that. Looking back now, I wonder if I didn't create the entire experience as a means of awakening me to this new experience of life. I had descended into a dream, that dream became a nightmare, and I forgot I had been sleeping. Now, my eyes had opened, and I saw the world as it was. It was a world filled with beauty; and it was perfect exactly as it was. When I was ready—and not a moment before—I was freed from the prison that held my body. This freedom did not come until I first freed myself from the prison that held my mind.

Charles Bynum

EPILOGUE

It has been three years now since I was released from prison. I sometimes wonder if it really happened—but then I know it did. The experience seems so distant now, as if it was a movie I watched a long time ago. I am often asked, "If you could go back, would you change anything? The answer to that, as remarkable as it may seem, is no. Everything happened exactly as it had to happen to bring me to where I needed to be. It was as if some invisible yet benevolent hand was gently guiding it all along, carrying me through each and every experience, knowing exactly what I needed and knowing exactly when I needed it. I journeyed through hell, and just as Ray had promised, I found heaven waiting for me on the other side. Then a most remarkable thing happened. I looked back to see where I had come from, only to find I was standing right where I started. The journey through hell was actually a journey away from my true nature. Heaven was within me all along.

I've heard it said, "It cannot be found by searching, but only those who search will find it." How true those words proved to be. It is the pathless path. We search in vain, for the truth we seek exists where it has always existed: in the center. Any path you choose can only lead you further away because you were already there before you ever began. So it cannot be found by searching. But search you must. Until, at long last, exhausted from the search itself, you stop trying. Then it finds you.

I have often said that getting out of prison was harder than going in. This may seem counter-intuitive, and in fact it seemed so to me. It was, nevertheless true. When you go to prison, your world shrinks drastically. Getting out, it expands just as drastically. This is a frightening experience. I remember the first time I walked into a Wal-Mart after my release. The sights, sounds and colors of the store are designed in such a way as to grab the attention of the shopper. For someone who had not experienced that in many years, the experience was overwhelming. It was an assault on my senses, and I simply could not handle it. I had to leave the store. It is funny how desensitized we have become.

I rode the bus out of prison with nineteen others being released that day. Of the twenty men on that bus, I am the only one who has not returned to county jail or prison. I do not say this to blow my own horn. I say this as an indictment of the system. I met many men who sincerely wanted to do well upon release, but they found the deck stacked horribly against them. The state gives you one-hundred dollars when you are released, and if you have nowhere to go, you are paroled to a sleazy crack and prostitute laden motel. Financial obligations of parole, and of simply trying to live life, mount quickly. Finding work is very difficult for a convicted felon. Many return to crime in an attempt to meet those obligations.

I was fortunate. I had a very supportive family who helped me through. My parents were there for me throughout my prison experience, and they continued to support me upon my release. I have often wondered how I would have made it without them. For those without such support, success upon release from prison is nearly impossible. It could be said that those who really want to succeed will, but that is far too simplistic an approach. It would be more accurate to say that many who wanted to succeed, and who put forth great effort to do so, failed because of an inadequate level of support. Society pays a heavy price for this.

On the other hand, I saw many men released from prison who had no desire whatsoever to change their behaviors. These men continued to cheat, lie, steal and rob with no remorse at all. Because of men such as these, I cannot blame those who want nothing to do with felons. Felons tend to be great liars. They are very charismatic and are good at fooling people. They prey on your trust, and they take advantage of that trust the minute they believe they have earned it. It is nearly impossible to distinguish between the sincere man trying to set his life straight, and the insincere one feigning sincerity in an attempt to rob you. There are no easy answers.

My life has continued to progress positively. Relationships with friends and family members that had been harmed as a result of my behaviors have begun to heal. Life is now something far better than I had ever imagined it could be. Every event of my journey was necessary to bring me to where I am today. I like who I am now, and my life is deeply rewarding in ways it never was, even before the madness.

I see now that every problem I ever had was born of one thing—selfishness. All suffering is ultimately derived from this. I now spend my life in the service of others—giving to others, caring for others, easing the suffering of others in whatever small ways I can. I once felt as if a void existed in the center of my being. I sought forever to fill it. I've learned that it can never be filled. It can be quieted for a moment, but soon it begins to long for more. When I turn that around and seek instead to give, that void is transformed into an infinite source, the fountainhead of infinite joy and beauty. Try to fill it, and it can never be filled. Give away what is in it, and it overflows with radiant abundance.

I have found that nothing in life is as important as I once thought it to be. As a result, I have stopped taking things so personally. Nothing is ever about me. Things just happen. I have stopped investing in the outcome of events, because therein lies the path to pain. Happiness is what happens when life does what I want; sorrow happens when life does other than what I want. The solution is not to alter life—that cannot be done. The solution is to stop *wanting*. This changed my perception of adversity. I no longer see adversity as something horribly unfair happening to me; I see it instead as life doing what life does. It therefore represents an opportunity to grow, to learn, to persevere. It is through the difficult times that we find our true strength. Without adversity, we would never be able to develop character.

I now look for what I can give to life, as opposed to worrying about what life can do for me. This is, I think, the most important distinction of all. Life didn't change, I did. I surrendered to life, and through that surrender began to accept everything in life exactly as it is. It was through that surrender that I found the thing we are all ultimately looking for—peace.

And so it was that I stumbled upon the left hand path. I've heard it said that the right hand path is the path most people choose. It is the path of societal conditioning. On such a path the individual lives out life conforming to the societal rules. The left hand path is one in which the individual breaks out of societal norms and forges his own way. This is the path of danger and uncertainty, yet it is the way to the realization of the true self.

www.ingramcontent.com/pod-product-compliance
Lightning Source LLC
Chambersburg PA
CBHW061644040426
42446CB00010B/1569